WATERSIDE DIARIES

WATERSIDE DIARIES

The wildlife observations of a
naturalist-angler

PROFESSOR
MARK EVERARD

HOBNOB PRESS

First published in the United Kingdom in 2025

by The Hobnob Press,
8 Lock Warehouse, Severn Road, Gloucester GL1 2GA
www.hobnobpress.co.uk

British Library Cataloguing in Publication Data
A catalogue record for this book is available from the British Library

ISBN 978-1-914407-85-7

Typeset in Doves Type.
Typesetting and origination by John Chandler

Printed by Lightning Source

CONTENTS

ABOUT THE AUTHOR

PROFESSOR MARK EVERARD is passionate about rivers, the living things within and beside them, and the many ways that they support our physical and mental health and life fulfilment.

Mark always wanted to play with water, ever since he was a small boy, and has contrived to live by and work with it ever since. Way back when the Earth was young, he completed his BSc (first class) in Freshwater and Marine Biology following by a PhD studying aspects of pollution in freshwater ecosystems. His subsequent studies and development work have taken him across Europe, Africa, South and East Asia, North America and Australia. This has included spending considerable time on water and ecosystem management in developing countries, where a little expertise can be beneficially applied to protect species, habitats and their capacities to support people.

Mark is a prolific author in scientific journals and magazines, and has also published 43 books at the time of writing. He is also a frequent contributor to television and radio. Mark's publications and other contributions cover aspects of ecosystems including wildlife, with a special interest in fish, as well as a breadth of sustainable development topics ranging from water management to the global food system and the sustainable use of chemicals. Mark has been a vocal and prominent environmental and sustainable development campaigner since the middle 1970s and intends to remain so until his last breath. He is an ambassador or science advisor to a wide range of conservation organisations in the UK, India and at intergovernmental level.

These scientific, campaigning and communications endeavours are driven by a foundational passion for water and the diversity of wildlife it supports from the microscopic to the gigantic, and the many functions that they perform underpinning biophysical, cultural and other aspects of human security and opportunity. Angling is, and has always been, a big part of Mark's life, work, writing and broadcasting, perhaps as a simple rationale for spending time by the river and becoming immersed in all the marvellous things that go on in and around it.

Waterside Diaries is the second in a series of books, the first titled Riverwatch, both of which began life as a series of articles that Mark has written for the local magazine Signpost distributed free to households in six villages in north Wiltshire through and around which the upper Bristol Avon runs. Modifications of many of these articles formed initial input to this book, before the writing process took on a life of its own.

Above all, Mark is a communicator about the wonders of the natural world, hoping to enthuse others about how fantastic, but above all how important, this awareness is for both its and our conjoined future wellbeing.

INTRODUCTION TO
WATERSIDE DIARIES

From my first memories, water attracted me like a moth to a flame. Or should that be a newt to a swamp? I could not pass by a puddle or even a bucket, a river or a pond, without an overwhelming desire to delve into the deep secrets that I felt it must hold. I always wanted to be by or in water, particularly flowing fresh water, but anything watery would suffice. This felt like the place I belonged.

After many decades and countless torrents of water flowing under the metaphorical bridge, nothing much has changed. I may have traded the perennially wet welly boots of those innocent days for a lifetime studying or otherwise working across five continents with water – also keeping fish, frogs and other beasties, scuba diving and angling whenever the slightest opportunity arose (or even when it didn't) – but the same flame still burns (if a flame can burn underwater). An unquenchable fascination with water remains the wellspring that keeps me inquiring, writing and broadcasting, campaigning and peering into puddles.

All of us are born of nature. We are also all composed by majority of water, and wholly reliant upon it for our security and life opportunities. This planet may be called Earth, but that is just the bit we stand on; the planetary surface is 70% water, and the atmosphere is a pale blue halo infused with and transporting prodigious quantities of moisture.

Time by water is healing, calming and inspiring. And, in its depths and its shallows, as well as emerging from it and coming to it to drink or breed, a kaleidoscope of living things reveals itself to the quiet observer.

Waterside Diaries captures just some of the myriad observations and reflections from the rippled surface as they shift with the turning of the seasons.

APRIL

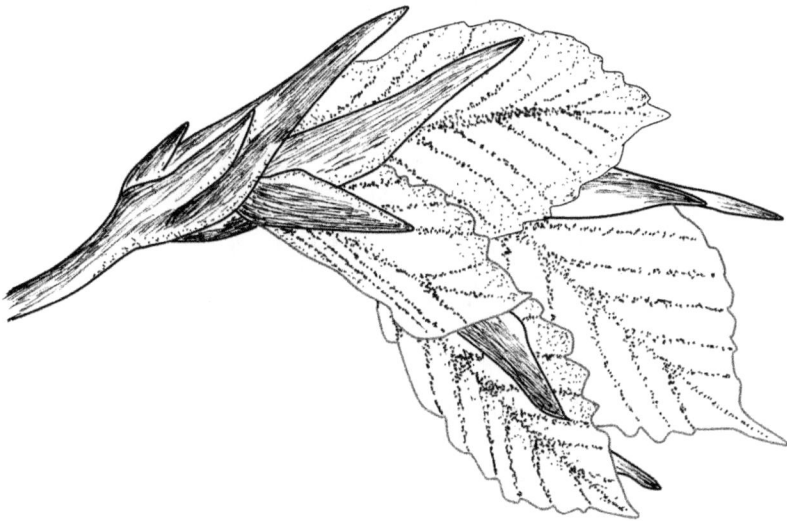

THE DAWN
SYMPHONY

F ROM THE END of March and through into the start of May, I love to
wake early to hear the sweetest of music seeping into our bedroom and
my dawning consciousness.

Starting at around 5:45 am in the early part of April, and progressively
earlier as daylength extends, the concerto invariably commences with the
mellifluous voice of a blackbird. First one, then another, and more join to
proclaim their territories from the tops of the trees and bushes that I can map
in my mind's eye in the near darkness.

The blackbird prelude is progressively augmented by the twittering and
fluting of robins and wrens, the choir swelling progressively as various tits,
warblers and other invisible and unnamed vocalists join the throng. Later in
the cycle, an increasingly scarce cuckoo may echo from the cover of a distant
wood. Often, the loudest amongst them is the disproportionately massive
vocalisation of the tiniest of wrens.

From sporadic fluting, the overture builds. It swells over long minutes, evolving into the central movement of full song. Then, progressively, the song cycle wanes after anything between a half-hour and a full hour, with often a momentary pause before the coarse crackle of rooks and the cooing of wood pigeons signal a segue into the sounds of full daytime.

As the daylight strengthens, other sounds of daytime take their place, including the flapping squabble of wood pigeons on the power line running in front of the house. The noises of busy humanity too increasingly intrude, breaking the spell of nature in largely uninterrupted finery.

From a crudely analytical perspective, the dawn chorus is little more than a mass clarion cry of sex and threat. Why would a potential prey animal announce itself so stridently to the wider world, if not for compelling reasons of survival? It is a cunning strategy to do so in the half-light when most sight-dependent predators, such as sparrowhawks, are at a disadvantage. However, it still entails risk. Bird songs, for all their beauty, are in the main an announcement staking a territorial claim on the new day as well as a call to potential mates at the outset of the breeding season.

But, in that delicious half-slumbering state on first waking, I am happy to allow my scientific mind a little rest and to float with the poets with the waxing and waning of the dawn symphony. From Chaucer to Bernard Shaw, poets have celebrated the dawn chorus, birdsong inspiring music in many forms from Vaughan Williams to Beethoven, Vivaldi and Benjamin Britten.

There is, in fact, an International Dawn Chorus Day set on the first Sunday of May, albeit that the preceding month is often the time of richest tunefulness. Framed as a worldwide celebration of nature's greatest symphony, International Dawn Chorus Day encourages people across the globe to rise early to experience the magnificence of the dawn soundscape. Many do so, though very many more do not, or at least do not intentionally, as the dawn chorus by that date starts around 4:30am. However, in reality, the 'International' tag is mainly a British invention as, down in the southern hemisphere, autumn is already processing at pace towards winter.

Whatever its biological functions and the tags that we humans put upon it, the dawn chorus is a thing of beauty and wonder. It is yet another free and invigorating gift from the natural world, and a balm for the soul that lightens whatever concerns may otherwise clamour for attention. To wake with the birds is a wonderful thing.

A BLIZZARD OF SEDGES

ONE OF THE many amazing sights on our rivers from the end of April or
into May, particularly on southern chalk rivers, is the mass emergence of
grannom flies.

The grannom (*Brachycentrus subnubilis*) is a sedge fly. 'Sedge fly'
is the common name of insects of the caddisfly family (order Trichoptera).
Caddisflies have aquatic larvae but terrestrial adults. They comprise
approximately 14,500 species worldwide. Adult caddisflies are small and
moth-like with two pairs of hairy membranous wings and long antennae.
They differ from moths in not having scales on their wings, and the wings are
folded back tent-like down the body when at rest.

The grannom is common in southern British rivers. It is one of the first
sedge flies to emerge in the year, typically from April with the main hatch
usually lasting for approximately ten days or so. The greatest concentration of
grannom taking to the wing occurs in and around weed beds. This location
is largely related to the fly's larval stage as, shortly after the egg hatches, the
emerging larva secretes silk from its salivary glands to surround itself in a
tubular case to which adjacent materials are glued. The grannom then remains
firmly attached to its host water plant throughout its larval and subsequent
pupal life.

Clouds of adult grannom can emerge in waves, generally from mid-
morning to mid-afternoon. This can be in such profusion on some chalk
rivers that they appear as a blizzard. At this time, this feast of grannom can

drive trout, grayling and other fish, as well as birds such as grey wagtails and warblers, into a feeding frenzy. Their synchronised emergence results in high mortality, but is dense enough to allow many insects to break free from the water's surface to fly up into the air. Once airborne, they generally take flight upstream to offset the tendency of downstream drift in the river.

Adult grannom have a dark, brownish-coloured body when they first emerge. Surviving emergers head for bankside cover such as streamside foliage and tree branches, as well as shaded areas such as under logs and rock ledges. Matured flies have a green-and-black barred body. Some mate while hanging upside down or clumped together. Many more matured grannom take flight from the undergrowth, returning to the river to mate and lay eggs.

After mating, the females develop an emerald-coloured egg sack, returning to the water to lay their eggs. Sometimes, they do this by flopping onto the water's surface, whilst others may dive underwater to deposit their eggs. After mating and egg-laying, grannom then die in their masses, ending up spent in the surface film, eagerly sipped in by feeding trout, grayling, chub, dace and other fishes, with profusions of dead flies sometimes forming mats in river slacks.

Eggs fall through the water column, ideally landing on submerged vegetation or other suitable surfaces. The larvae attach and live an aquatic life for a year. When fully grown, grannom larvae then pupate in situ. When emerging, the pupae break free of their cases, potentially drifting for several feet before beginning their ascent to the surface. Once in the surface film, it can take them up to 30 minutes to emerge as full-fledged adults, often crawling up emergent stems and branches before taking to the air. This aerial emergence from bankside vegetation is the origin of the common name 'sedge fly'. This is, of course, yet another vulnerable time.

Clearly, it is important that the submerged vegetation to which grannom larvae and pupae attach persists throughout the year. For this reason, the greatest abundance of grannom is found in southern chalk rivers that are fed by groundwater, conferring on them a stable temperature regime across the seasons allowing water plants to grow profusely.

Grannom are just one of the approximately 200 species of sedge flies found in Britain, encompassing a great diversity of larval life stages adapted to ponds, temporary water bodies, powerful rivers and more gentle flows.

The larvae of some species of caddis, as is well known, form cases of stones, sand, vegetation or other material surrounding their bodies. Many are mobile, trundling around on the river or pool bed like little aquatic caravans. Others are caseless and these are often mobile predators. Some, like grannon, stick their cases permanently to an underwater surface.

Look out for the emergence of these small, dusty-looking flies towards late afternoon; they are a joy to watch and an indicator of river health!

RED IN BEAK AND WEBBED FEET

WITH APRIL UPON us, we are likely to be seeing the appearance of small flotillas of fluffy ducklings. Each of these tight groups will be shepherded by a vigilant female, the youngsters initially staying close to her at the command of her persistent sibilance and gently maternal, though occasionally more alarmed, quacking.

These ducklings are charming little creatures, all soft brown and yellow fluff with their downy chick feathers, precociously able to swim right from hatching out in waterside nests.

Yet they are also born killers! We will all have seen a duckling bursting out from the tight cluster to chase a fly: all gawky limbs, stubby wings and splashy movement powered by madly paddling feet. But this is no juvenile game driven by curiosity. It is in fact essential for survival as each of these cute youngsters has to get a protein boost from animal matter if it is to grow on strongly enough to withstand life's rigours. Without mixing carnivory – flies, worms, other mainly invertebrate matter and, opportunistically, small fish and fish eggs – with otherwise vegetative fare, the ducklings are likely to succumb to any of a wide range of pressures, or simply to die.

One cool spring day in March, I saw the largest family of mallard ducklings that I have ever seen. The mother duck was guiding her eighteen freshly hatched youngsters around the boats moored on the far bank of the canal, to the admiring gaze and much cooing from passing walkers on the towpath. But the sad reality, as I saw it, was that most or all were destined to die. This early, and without the prospect of early emergence of sufficient chironomid and other flies from still-cold water further chilled by a persistent easterly air stream, there would be insufficient suitable animal protein available for them to build up the body tissues necessary to withstand the cold and the attentions of predators.

One of the reasons that many ducks have such large broods (twelve ducklings or more in a brood is quite common for a mallard), and that some have multiple broods in a year, is that each duckling is a tasty and nutritious morsel for a range of predators. Perhaps the greatest threat for ducklings comes from black-backed gulls – the lesser black-back gull (*Larus fuscus*) inland joined by the great black-backed gull (*Larus marinus*: the largest British member of the gull family) nearer the coast – these voracious birds always alert as they survey springtime water bodies from above to pick off stragglers. But other birds, including herons, will opportunistically take a duckling. Even other female ducks brooding their own youngsters may kill a duckling from another brood that strays too close to her entourage, and swans too can kill ducklings. Neither ducks nor swans eat the duckling's body. Below the water, the predatory pike will readily take a duckling, ambushing it from below in a sudden and violent swirl of water. Even ostensibly non-predatory fish species can take a duckling small enough to fit in their mouths, large common carp well able to swallow a duckling from beneath the water's surface. And, of course, we have mammals such as otters and mink that can take ducklings in the water, as well as badgers and foxes that may intercept them on the bank. The list of enemies of the duckling, each evolved to further their own survival, is long indeed.

Life on, by and in our rivers is precarious. All life forms comprising the river ecosystem follow their own strategies to feed, evade, and to ensure that sufficient progeny survive to perpetuate their lineage. But all are also elements of nature's immense and magnificent machinery of closely conjoined and evolved cogs, co-dependent upon each other and the sustainability of the greater cycles of the natural world.

In this grander scheme of things, no natural creature is hero or villain, all having tightly evolved roles to play. Even those ever-so-cute ducklings, all charm and Easter card charisma, conceal their true nature: "Red in tooth and claw" as Alfred, Lord Tennyson put it, though "Red in beak and webbed feet" might be more apt in this instance.

THE BLACKTHORN
WINTER

A s March segues into early April, the hedgerows frost white with
cool blossom bursting from bare twigs. Clusters of buds swell,
initially showing tight masses of white tips like tiny constellations. These
subsequently explode into a froth of long-petalled blossoms appearing at first
as a scattered few but, within the week, the field margins appear at a distance
as if holding hoar frost all day. And this all before the new hawthorn leaves
have yet to unfurl to paint the hedges with their new, soft green hue.

Generally, this fog of white presages a cool snap of weather, chilled
further on the changing season's blustering winds. Early in the day, the
hoar frost is often far more than just a floral illusion. This is the 'blackthorn
winter', reminding us of the reluctance of the receding winter to loosen its
icy grip. All the while, waves of freshly emergent shoots – cleavers, cuckoo
pint, cow parsley and hemlock amongst them – lap the base of the still barren
shrubbery, a rising vernal tide.

The name of the blackthorn is literal, descriptive of the dark bark with
pointed, thorn-like spur shoots. It is this same bush or small tree, naturally
common across Europe, western Asia and locally in northwest Africa though

introduced beyond this range, from which later in the year we find sloes. Sloes are best collected after the first frost of autumn, or else used after time in a freezer, after which their astringency is reduced. They are famously used along with sugar to make sloe gin, with sloe vodka a popular alternative.

Sloes are also used in other regional drinks, including pacharán in Navarre, Spain, as well as bargnolino in Italy, and eau de vie de prunelle in regions of France including Alsace. In France also, a similar drink known as épine (or épinette or troussepinette) is made from young blackthorn shoots harvested in spring and immersed in wine. Wine made from fermented sloes is also made in Britain, Germany and other central European countries.

Sloes can also be made into jam, chutney and used in fruit pies. Juice extracted from sloes has been used as a reddish dye for linen, washing out to a durable pale blue. The leaves of the blackthorn, resembling those of the tea plant, and have also been used as an addition to tea. There are also historical records of blackthorn sap being used as an ingredient in the production of inks.

The wood of the blackthorn is put to a range of uses. As a fuelwood, blackthorn produces good heat with little smoke. The wood can also be polished to a fine finish, and blackthorn staves are put to a variety of uses including as handles for tools as well as straight canes traditionally used to make walking sticks or clubs (known in Ireland as shillelagh). Blackthorn sticks are also carried by commissioned officers of the Royal Irish Regiment in the British Army as well as in Irish regiments in some Commonwealth countries. Owing to its long, sharp thorns, blackthorn has also traditionally been used in Britain and other parts of northern Europe to make cattle-proof hedges.

The blackthorn tree (*Prunus spinosa*) is hardy and related to other species of plum (various species of the genus *Prunus*). Consequently, blackthorn is also used as rootstock onto which shoots of other species of plum and some other fruit trees are grafted.

It is not just people that make use of blackthorn. The leaves of this deciduous shrub or small tree serve as a food plant for the larvae of a wide range of moths and butterflies. One moth caterpillar, the concealer moth (*Esperia oliviella*), feeds on dead blackthorn wood.

This and much more natural and cultural wealth is associated with the blackthorn, for which the inconvenience of a few days of chilly weather during the 'blackthorn winter' is a small price to pay.

WELCOMING THE RETURN OF THE RED AEROBAT

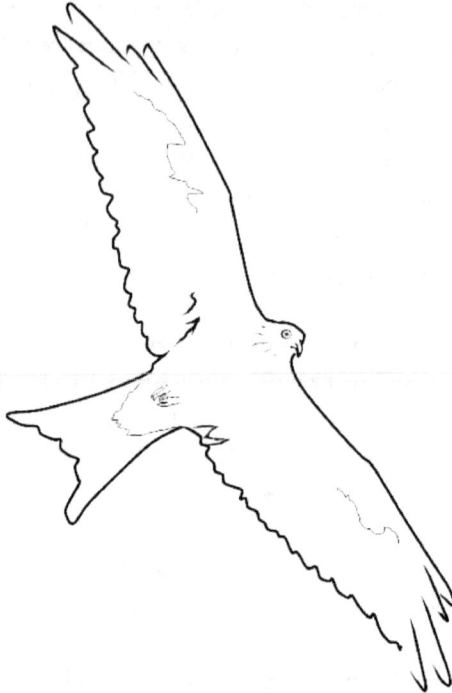

A CERTAIN RED aerobatic master has become an increasingly common sight over river valleys, hills and wider landscapes across Britain.

The red kite (*Milvus milvus*) is a majestic flyer on broad wings that can span five feet. The distinctively forked tail flexes constantly to finely orient the bird, making it a very agile flyer indeed. The 'red' part of the bird's name derives from its reddish-brown and black-streaked plumage. Red kites are true aerobats; masters of the air that are not easily confused with buzzards which soar on more rounded wings and tails.

The fortunes of red kites have been distinctly variable over recent centuries. During the 19th century, serial persecution had driven the bird to extinction throughout most of the United Kingdom except for a small surviving population in Wales. By then, red kites had also been extirpated from several countries across the western Palearctic, their native range, following a marked long-term decrease in range and numbers. (The western Palearctic is one of the planet's eight ecozones encompassing terrestrial ecoregions of Europe, Asia north of the Himalayan foothills, northern Africa, and the northern and central parts of the Arabian Peninsula.)

However, red kites were once common across Britain, where they were often considered an urban bird much as the black kite is today in Asian and African cities. The red kite was a valued scavenger in Britain during the Middle Ages. Recognising its role in keeping streets clean, this bird was protected by royal decree; the killing of a kite was a capital offence.

Times and attitudes changed. By the 16th century, a bounty was placed on the head of the red kite, as indeed on many birds of prey, leading to their relentless persecution as 'vermin'. Game keepers were ruthless in persecution of the kite, wrongly accusing it of taking game. With increasing rarity, red kites were targeted by taxidermists and egg collectors serving a growing trade. These actions hastened the extinction of the bird in England in 1871, and in Scotland in 1879. By 1903, only a handful of pairs were left in remote parts of central Wales. However, from that time, they began to receive protection.

Happily, the fortunes for this elegant bird have changed once again. Over recent decades, the red kite has been successfully reintroduced into England and Scotland with some striking results. A reintroduction programme was set up in 1989 by the Royal Society for the Protection of Birds (RSPB) and the (then) Nature Conservancy Council, recognising that the slow population expansion in Wales meant that natural recolonisation of other suitable parts of the Britain from Wales or continental Europe was unlikely.

In England, red kites have been successfully reintroduced to four areas: the Chilterns, East Midlands, Yorkshire and north-east England. The first birds were brought from Spain. However, the Chilterns population grew quickly enough to enable small numbers of young birds to be donated to establish populations in the other areas. The 'Northern Kites' reintroduction project near Gateshead began in 2004. Red kites were also introduced from Sweden and Germany into North and Central Scotland, where breeding populations have since been successfully established. A further reintroduction of 100 red kites from the Chilterns and North Scotland has resulted in the bird now also establishing breeding populations in Dumfries and Galloway.

Key to the success of these reintroductions has been education of landowners and gamekeepers that red kites pose no risk to game shooting interests or livestock. In fact, for all their aerial dexterity, red kites are ground feeders, with a diet principally of carrion. However, they can kill some small live prey such as birds and small mammals, also feeding on invertebrates such as earthworms or slugs, onto which they dive from the air or drop from a perch. Where they now inhabit or visit urban areas, red kites will scavenge refuse tips and visit gardens where meat scraps are put out for them, returning to the scavenging habits of the Middle Ages for which they were famed and valued.

Now, many landowners are proud to have red kites nesting on their land, contributing to monitoring and protection of the bird. Local economies too have benefited, with 'kite country' green tourism, 'red kite trials' and other initiatives established in various parts of the country, and some enterprising farmers setting up kite-feeding stations that draw in large numbers of visitors.

So, if you see this elegant aerobat soaring on its long wings, please welcome it back with good wishes and gratitude that it has recovered from ill treatment in our less enlightened past.

MAY

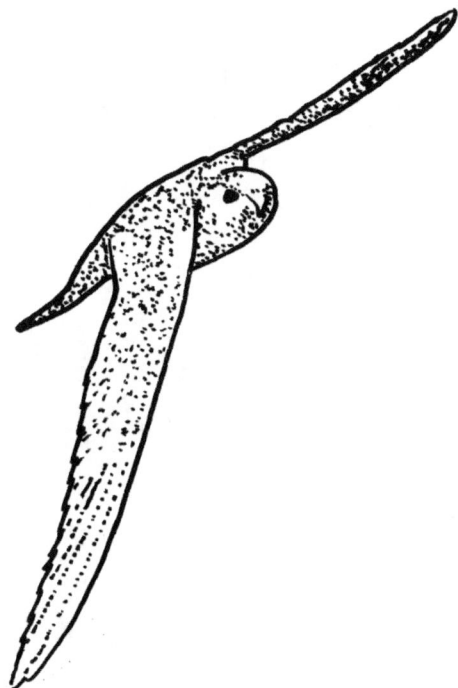

UNCORKING OF THE SPRINGTIME BOTTLE

T O SOME PEOPLE, they are unwelcome 'weeds'.
    To me, they are a potent symbol of spring in unfettered, frothy
splendour. I love the vista of white foam created by innumerable umbelliferous
heads held aloft, high and proud above verges, riverbanks and the margins
of hedgerows and copses. This is the uncorking of the bottle of suppressed
springtime energy, bursting up above the lower sward of early season promise.

Cow parsley (*Anthriscus sylvestris*) is a common umbellifer found across
lowland Britain, as well as various parts of Europe, Asia and Africa. The
plant is a native biennial or short-lived perennial, flowering from April to June.
Its dissected, fern-like leaves are some of the earliest to emerge after winter in
low swards though, as spring progresses, it shoots up hollow, furrowed stems
bearing flattened umbels (umbrella-like) comprising panicles of small, white
flowers. Often, the flower stems can be purple-tinged.

Cow parsley is also known by a variety of other local names, including
wild beaked parsley, wild chervil, Queen Anne's lace, and keck. Other
reported names apparently include mother-die as well as devil's parsley, the
reasons for which may be, as we will see, due to its potential confusion with
close relatives rather than the cow parsley itself.

Cow parsley is one of the earliest-flowering of Britain's ten native umbelliferous plants. These include, for example, hogweed, hemlock, hemlock water dropwort, hogweed and pepper saxifrage. However, cow parsley tends to die back quickly after producing seeds.

Ecologically, cow parsley is important as an early source of nectar for pollinators and other beneficial insects, which are fed on in turn by other wildlife including returning swallows and house martins as well as a range of other animals. Cow parsley leaves are also a food plant for some moth caterpillars, including for example the double square-spot (*Xestia triangulum*) and the single-dotted wave (*Idaea dimidiate*). Cow parsley flowers are attractive to orange-tip butterflies, marmalade hoverflies and a range of other insects. The seeds are also used as food by a range of small rodents. Some insects, including earwigs, can make use of their dried, hollow stems to shelter over winter. Rabbits are particularly fond of grazing on cow parsley leaves.

Human uses of cow parsley are various. When cow parsley is crushed between the fingers, the leaves produce a strong, aniseed-like scent in common with many members of the carrot family. Although cow parsley is edible with a flavour between mild aniseed and liquorice, and in fact is still eaten in various forms by some people, this is not advisable for the non-expert as it is similar and often found in proximity to potentially deadly related plants including hemlock and hemlock water dropwort.

Cow parsley has been used in traditional medicines, addressing ailments ranging from stomach and kidney problems, breathing difficulties and colds, as a digestive aid and for lowering high blood pressure. It also has a long history of use as a mosquito repellent. Reportedly, the leaves and stems of the plant have anti-inflammatory, antibacterial, antioxidant, antiseptic, antispasmodic, anti-epileptic, antiviral and fungistat properties, amongst a range of attributed properties, although I cannot vouch for their efficacy or safety.

In addition to human herbal uses, cow parsley has also been used for veterinary purposes. Horses seem to have a particular appetite for cow parsley, which is said to have similar properties to fennel in aiding digestion, possessing calmative properties and speeding healing processes. If the range of properties attributed to cow parsley in human and equine herbal medicine has any validity, the plant is likely to confer other benefits to other animals.

We are, today, used to seeing farm animals fed on monocultures of fast-growing grass strains, such as perennial ryegrass (*Lolium perenne*). This may maximise production of biomass, but the diet lacks diversity. Naturally, animals including the progenitors of modern livestock would have grazed on species-rich grasslands containing cow parsley with its diversity of medicinal qualities, clover that rebuilds the nitrogen content of the soil, many herbs with antihelminthic (ridding the body of parasitic worms) and other parasite-suppressing properties, and a host of other natural nutrients and therapeutic and restorative properties. Today, our intensively monoculture-fed livestock has to be given regular nutritional supplements and veterinary medicines to maintain health and optimise growth. Have we perhaps lost something in our input-intensive maximisation of productivity? Have we lost sight of the many benefits that accrue from grazing on naturally diverse meadows and other sources of food, which may provide a wealth of nutrients and pest management measures on a far more sustainable, potentially lower-cost, basis?

Weed or not, I welcome cow parsley as an effusive symbol of spring having well and truly sprung, and as a symbol of traditional wisdoms that we may have set aside but that will certainly be vital to rekindle as we seek a more sustainable pathway into the future.

BANDED AND BEAUTIFUL

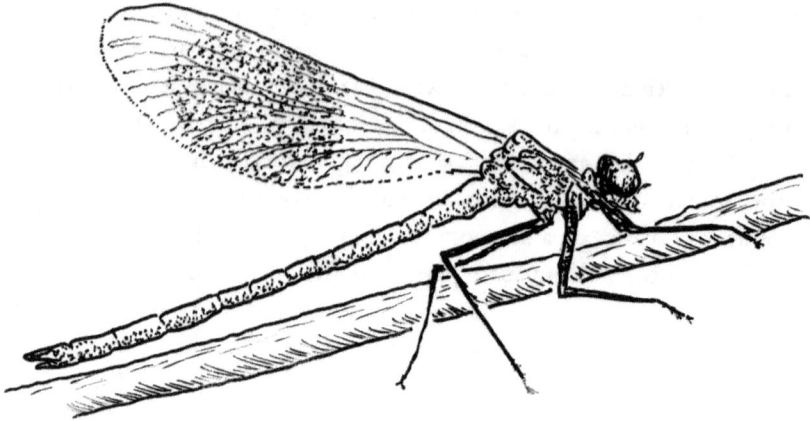

D URING THE MONTH of May, and most profusely from the warmer
days towards the end of the month, the waterside may be charmed by
the emergence and dance of the demoiselles.

'Demoiselle' literally means 'young lady'. And, if the #METOO
generation will forgive it, the metaphor for the balletic flight of brightly hued
demoiselle flies emerging on the wing seems more apt than if they were named,
say, 'front row rugby player flies'.

As many scuba divers and other fishy enthusiasts may know, the various
species of marine damselfish are also known as 'demoiselles' in French. Clouds
of gaudy fish parading around rocky reefs in clear and warm water evoke
rather more the grace of the ballerina than of the bricklayer.

Many of the rivers of lowland Britain are blessed with two species of
demoiselle flies, both living out their lives as aquatic larvae for one or two years
before taking to the wing when spring is well progressed.

The banded demoiselle (*Calopteryx splendens*) is a relatively large insect,
about 4.5 centimetres or one-and-three-quarters inches long with a metallic-
coloured body. In mid- to late-spring and into mid-summer, the larvae climb
up out of the water, generally on plant stems, the back of the larval 'skin' then
splitting to enable the fully winged adult demoiselle to climb out, dry off and

take to the air in all its glory. The male banded demoiselle is metallic blue and characterised by the 'bands' of its name, a distinctive dark band running across both the two pairs of wings. By contrast, the female banded demoiselle is a shiny green and has no banding on the wings.

The other species that may be commonly encountered is the beautiful demoiselle (*Calopteryx virgo*). Superficially similar to the banded demoiselle, adult male beautiful demoiselles have dark-coloured wings without distinct bands and their bodies are metallic blue-green. Females have brown wings and with metallic green bodies.

In general, the beautiful demoiselle prefers more rapidly flowing water whereas the banded demoiselle is more often seen near still or sluggish flowing water, though the distributions of both insects overlap. Around our home reaches of river in North Wiltshire, both species seem to fare well alongside each other.

Whilst both the banded and beautiful demoiselles may look like dragonflies, they are in fact large damselflies. Their flight pattern certainly has more in common with damselflies than the agile aerobatics of the generally larger and far more robust dragonflies. But do not let their flitting and fluttering flight pattern fool you. Both species predate on other smaller flying insects, and the pirouetting flight is also deployed by male insects seeking to attract and impress passing females with their dance moves.

For much of the time, demoiselles rest on bankside vegetation, in particular the males as they await passing females.

The aquatic larvae of both British demoiselle species have long bodies, three short spikey caudal lamellae (gills extending beyond the rear of the body) and long horn-like antennae on the heads. Eggs are deposited into the water by adult female insects, hatching after between 20 to 30 days. Damselfly larvae are predatory, feeding on a variety of smaller aquatic insect larvae and other small invertebrates. They undergo between 10 and 12 instars (phases between moulting exoskeletons) and may remain in the larval stage over one or two winters before emerging as mature adults.

Beautiful or banded, these magnificent insects brighten the waterside, particularly on sunnier and stiller days, when they emerge to take to the wing as gaudy adults from May to August.

FLAGS FLYING

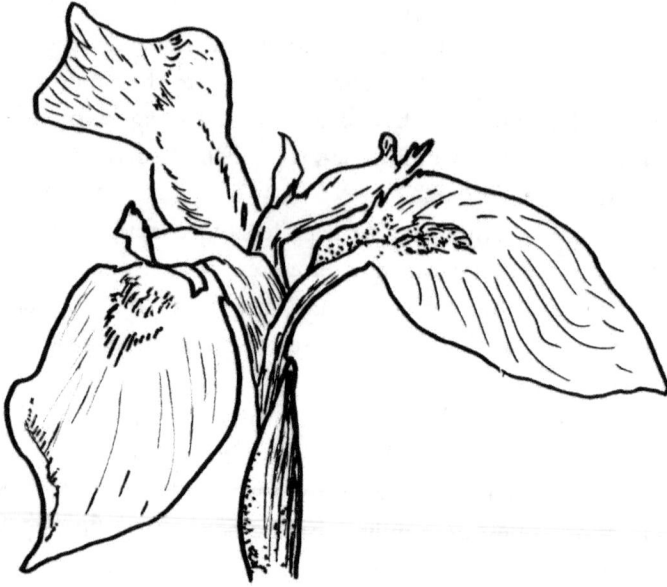

THE BANKS OF rivers and pools as well as swamps and other wetlands,
including some ditches, are a panorama of living wonders as spring
unfurls its bright flags. One bright yellow flag in particularly brightens the
bankside in this month.

The yellow flag iris is familiar to almost all of us who walk riverbanks
and around the margins of lakes in late spring. Stands of flattened blades,
springing from the dank waterside earth from March onwards, have reached
their greatest height and, held aloft amongst and above them, are the gaudy
flower heads of the yellow flag.

The yellow flag iris (*Iris pseudacorus*) is also commonly known as yellow
iris, or flag iris. Other local names include 'segg' or 'sword-grass', the latter
referring to its blade-like leaves. It is a tall plant up to a metre-and-a-half
high, with distinctive yellow flowers opening from May but through to July
in cooler climes. The plant is common throughout the British Isles except for
the Highlands of Scotland, occurring on wet and boggy soils along river and
pond margins and in some wet woodlands. It can also withstand a moderate
level of salinity, and so also appears in some estuaries. The plant spreads

by rhizomes (underground stems much like those of the yellow water lily or stinging nettle), and so often forms dense patches. However, it also sets seeds in the autumn. These dark-stacked, disc-like seeds form in elongated pods once the flowers have been fertilised. Once the pods dry and split, the buoyant seeds tumble out and wash away, those landing opportunistically on favourable soils distributing the plant.

The yellow flag is in the family Iridaceae, the irises, and is native to Europe, western Asia and northwest Africa. However, in some regions where the plant is not native, including the USA and South Africa, yellow flag has escaped from cultivation to establish itself as an invasive aquatic plant which can create dense, monotypic stands outcompeting other plants in the ecosystem. Sale of the plant is banned in some of these non-native ranges, though it is still widely sold in other non-native regions for use in gardens with all the problems that this practice potentially raises.

When the flowers open, they are highly attractive not just to the human eye but also to bees that rely on them for nectar and that help transfer pollen from flower to flower. Nectar production by the yellow flag flower is very high, making the plant an important seasonal food source for bees and other pollinating insects. The six parts of the flower in fact comprise three petals and three sepals (flower bud coverings), all brightly coloured with that characteristic and vivid tone of yellow.

Like many of our waterside and other plants, the yellow flag iris has formerly been put to many uses. One use has been as an extract from the rhizomes producing black dye and black ink. The plant has also been used in traditional medicine as an astringent helping control blood flow though, consumed in excess, the plant is also considered mildly toxic. The roasted seeds have also reportedly been used to make a coffee-like drink.

The yellow flag also has significant cultural meanings. One of these is that the yellow iris is thought by some people to be inspiration of the 'fleur-de-lis' (French for 'lily flower') symbol widely appearing in heraldry. A stylised rendition of the yellow flag iris on a blue background is also depicted as the flag of the Brussels-Capital Region. This is perhaps related to the iris featuring on the sceptre of the descendants of Charlemagne, including Charles of France who set up a fortified camp in the area in the Duchy of Lower Lotharingia. This choice of site as a capital is considered the foundation of Brussels. In Ireland, bunches of yellow flag are hung outside doors on the Feast of Corpus Christi in the belief that they ward off evil. The yellow iris has also been

chosen as the County Flower of Wigtownshire, perhaps as the county's
marshy hollows are often flooded with its bright 'flags'.

The yellow flag is said to have played a significant role in a key victory
by the Duke of Brabant, ruler of the Duchy of Brabant from 1183/1184. (The
Duchy of Brabant, across the low countries of continental Europe much
of which is now in the modern-day Netherlands, was created by the Holy
Roman Emperor Frederick Barbarossa in favour of Henry I.) Knowing the
plant could only grow in shallow water, the Duke's troops used iris-covered
areas to mark a safe passage enabling them to gallop through the flooded
plains; their opponents who were not so aware becoming bogged down in the
marshes.

OUT OF THIN AIR

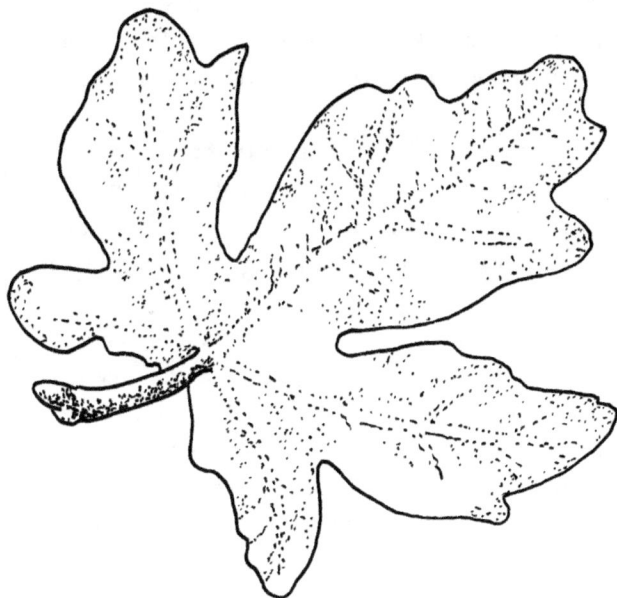

LOOKING AT A leaf on a tree, I am impressed that it has materialised out of thin air.

The alchemy of photosynthesis harnesses energy from light to split hydrogen atoms from water molecules, fusing them with carbon dioxide from the air to create sugars that then form the basis of myriad other complex organic substances. The carbon skeleton and processing machinery of the leaf is literally drawn from air.

So too the substance of the vista of grasses I see from my window, not only in the garden by across the landscape of the wide river valley. And, looking at satellite imagery of the globe's green cover, all of that too. All created from thin air.

The weighty, robust structure of trees as well. Wood is built from the products of photosynthesis, from the sapling to the mighty standard oaks that have stood resolute and resistant to storms over lifespans of centuries. The wood in the door next to which I am sitting right now also began life as gases circulating in the atmosphere. The timbers of galleons, timber-framed houses, furniture and other durable edifices were also constructed by plants from thin air, as too the paperwork all around me and the cardboard boxes and files within which much of it resides.

My gaze and appreciation are broadened and enriched by this new vista of the universe I inhabit. I recognise too the clothes I am wearing and the carpet beneath my feet as structures initially created from thin air, expressed by plants as cotton or moderated after ingestion by animals into wool and other fibres.

Living adjacent to the Oolitic limestone of the Cotswolds, the very ground beneath my feet is also formed by carbonates initially locked from the air and fed into complex and ancient natural cycles. The same is true of the 'tilth' of the soil: its organic content imbuing it with fertility and a capacity to retain water.

Even the plastics all around me – in domestic appliances, luggage, computer casings, my phone and other electronic equipment, the profiles of my windows and so much more – started life as the products of photosynthesis, the carbon harvested by long-dead plants now forming the backbones of synthetic molecules from the oil reserve into which this ancient productivity was transformed by heat and pressure by majority in the Mesozoic age (252 to 66 million years ago). Plucking the nylon strings of my guitar, the sound is generated by the vibration of the material of the string and the resonance of wood fibre comprising the guitar's body, both synthesised from carbon chains built from thin air captured in forests hundreds of millions of years in the past.

And, of course, my car is powered by energy falling on the Earth in the Carboniferous period of Earth's evolution, from the end of the Devonian Period and the beginning of the Permian Period (roughly 358.9 - 298.9 million years ago), locked up within the carbon bonds of complex molecules. Igniting the petrochemicals in air splits apart these carbon bonds, releasing ancient energy to propel me to my destination and leaving behind traces of the ancient atmosphere from which it was extracted.

When the Earth was forming as a protoplanet some 4.5 billion years ago, it lacked structure as a condensing gas cloud. All manner of processes separated and segregated matter to form the discrete principal environmental media – earth, water and air – with which we are familiar today. Carbon dioxide was abundant in the early atmosphere, producing a greenhouse effect (trapping infrared energy re-emitted from incident solar energy much as a greenhouse operates) that made planetary temperature far too extreme for water to exist in liquid state. A cooling planet enabled the condensation of water and, eventually, the genesis of life, the evolution and processes of which vastly accelerated the accretion of carbon-rich substances into a growing planetary crust. And so, in a deep historical context, we live today in an atmosphere of low carbon dioxide concentration, lowered in substantial measure through the accelerating impact of millennia of vegetative activity drawing carbon out of thin air to form living and non-living structures.

It is salient to reflect on the folly of the contemporary substantial rates of extraction of carbon sequestered in all its forms at minuscule pace over geological timescales, now liberated *en masse* into an atmosphere that is now heating and incrementally returning to more life-hostile and unstable stages of planetary evolution.

All this and more by simply reflecting on a leaf, busy unhurriedly producing structure, life-giving substances and embodied energy out of thin air.

REBELS WITH A CAUSE

I T IS LIFE-AFFIRMING to walk the pathways along rivers, field margins, hills and woods. Popular too: outdoor recreation was estimated to be the favourite national pastime in 2013, 75% of adults enjoying it at least monthly and 51% weekly.

One of the things that visitors to the countryside of our islands often remark is just how liberated we are. There are plenty of places to walk, across farmed and other land in both private and public ownership. And, so long as we respect the rights of way, we are a less restricted people than many across continental Europe, the USA and many other parts of the world. Whilst the 'right to roam' is not as absolute as some believe, we do enjoy access to greener places to a remarkable extent compared to many countries. Perhaps we do not appreciate often enough how lucky we are, and how our relative freedoms came to be. So, as you perambulate in accessible places, spare a thought for the rebels that made this everyday pleasure possible.

At dawn on 24th April 1932, 400 working-class ramblers from Manchester and Sheffield set out to reach Kinder Scout in the Peak District. This was no mere 'walk in the park', enjoyed as a common right. Rather, it was a wilful and coordinated act of civil disobedience, deliberately confronting the Duke of Derbyshire's gamekeepers and the police. The ramblers were staking a claim for the right to roam, contesting the exclusive grouse-shooting rights of the landowners.

One group started from Hayfield in the west; another from Edale in the east. Scuffles broke out with gamekeepers, some reports claiming at least some 'gamekeepers' were hired thugs. However, despite the arrest of some trespassers, the blockade failed to stop the groups converging on Kinder Scout's plateau.

This walk in the countryside made national headlines, attracting public attention and political support. It led on to successive events and waves of support, amplifying public demand for the right to access to our famed 'green and pleasant land' that was, in reality, held in private and exclusive hands. A series of bills granting public access to mountains and other valued landscapes was to follow, legislation from the National Parks and Access to the Countryside Act 1949 to the Countryside and Rights of Way (CROW) Act 2000 formalising a 'right to roam' in certain areas of England and Wales. The CROW Act 2000 grants the public a right to depart from limited rights of way only on designated 'access land', though not on horseback or cycle. It is certainly not a carte blanche on all land as some mistakenly construe it.

The 1949 Act also enabled designation of specific areas as National Parks. In 1951, the Peak District, possibly by no coincidence, became the UK's first National Park. Most recently, in 2010, the South Downs became the nation's fifteenth. Today, National Parks cover almost 10% of the UK's land area, encompassing mountains, chalk streams, wetlands and coastlines. Footpaths, bridleways and bye-ways reticulate our streams, woodland and farmland, enabling us common people to access and enjoy these treasured, inspiring and regenerative landscapes and waterscapes.

The mass trespass profoundly changed the course of environmentalism and civil rights in the UK, ultimately gifting us many of the freedoms we take as given today; freedoms of access that are still not entrenched in many other nations around the world.

Establishment in 1899 of the UK's first nature reserve at Wicken Fen in Cambridgeshire was an early precursor of a movement that accelerated rapidly in the post-Second World War period, as society grew more empowered and aware, contesting the destructive trends of Victorian industrialisation and loss of countryside. The social and environmental strands of this movement cannot be disentangled, as people began increasingly to express concern not only about degradation of the natural environment but also about how the benefits that it confers on society are shared by all, rather than appropriated for the exclusive enjoyment of a select few. As more countryside subsequently became accessible, the diversity of outdoor pursuits and freedoms blossomed.

Public 'rights of way' of course existed prior to this wider opening of the countryside, many of them ancient though now enshrined in legally protected rights to pass on foot, bicycle or horseback. There are also permissive paths, not formally designated, where landowners grant access rights.

We should nonetheless be ever mindful of and grateful to those 'rebels with a cause' that made possible the freedoms we enjoy today, whilst remaining respectful of the ecology and livelihoods supported by these wilder places.

JUNE

LION'S TEETH

L OVE THEM (SPRINGTIME bees do) or hate them (notably some gardeners
and groundkeepers), the dandelion is one tough and amazing plant!

Bright yellow dandelion flowers, 1-2 inches (2½ to 5 centimetres) across,
are a near-constant presence in grasslands from March to October, the longest
flowering season of any of our native plants. Their bright flower heads open
to greet the morning, closing again in the evening.

The dandelion is also said to represent three celestial bodies: the sun
through its bright yellow flowers; the moon in the 'puff ball' of feathery seeds;

and the stars as the seeds are borne aloft on summer breezes by their downy parachutes and to travel as far as five miles.

The dandelion is also a most useful plant. Its roots, leaves and flowers are all put to work as food, drink, medicine and a source of dye.

The leaves, serrated on their edges, give the plant its French name Dent de Lion ('lion's teeth'), from which we derive the word 'dandelion'. They can be blanched and eaten as an addition to salad or as a fresh vegetable. In Asian cooking, dandelion leaves are used like lettuce, boiled, made into soup or fried. Dandelion flower buds can be added to omelettes and fritters, the flowers may be baked into cakes, and the pollen can be sprinkled on food for decoration and colouring.

The stout tap root can be dried and ground for use as a coffee substitute, and for making root beer. Dandelion flowers are also used for making wine, and beer can be brewed from the whole plant before it flowers. Dandelion-and-burdock is a popular and distinctively flavoured fizzy drink made in the north of England, occasionally appearing in shops throughout the country.

Like the plant itself, the medicinal properties of the dandelion also have long roots. They were well-known to ancient Egyptians, Greeks and Romans, and the plant has been used in Chinese traditional medicine for over a thousand years. Dandelion has also been used in European folk medicine to treat infections and liver disorders. Tea made of infused dandelions acts as diuretic.

The yellow flowers of the dandelion can be dried and ground into a yellow-pigmented powder and used as a dye. Dandelions also secrete a latex when tissues are cut or broken, low in yield in wild strains but increased in some cultivated strains, that has found uses as a natural source of rubber of the same quality as that exuded from rubber trees.

A number of Western traditions are also associated with the dandelion seed head. For some, the number of times you blow across a dandelion 'clock' head until all the seeds fly off will tell you the time of day. For others, thinking of a wish when blowing off the seeds is thought to make that wish come true.

In fact, so useful was the dandelion that, at least up until the 1800s, people remove grass from lawns to better enable the growth of useful plants including dandelions, chickweed, malva and chamomile; an interesting historical observation given the substantial expenditure of time, effort and money that many gardeners and groundsmen expend today to remove them to create pristine lawns!

The dandelion plant is extremely important for wildlife too. As a season-long source of nectar, dandelions provide a valuable early-season feast for bees, butterflies and many other insects. They do so throughout their long flowering season. Various birds also eat dandelion seeds in season. Rabbits and other grazing animals also eat this plant, which draws up nutrients from deep underground through its long tap root. Lying low in meadow swards, and growing and regenerating from a rosette from the top of the tap root, dandelions are resistant to grazing and trampling. This is a virtue in a wildlife setting, if a bane to the tidy gardener as, when mowed persistently, dandelions simply grow shorter stalks!

'Dandelion' in fact refers to any plant in the genus *Taraxacum*, native to Eurasia and North America. The species *Taraxacum officinale* is most familiar to us in the British Isles. In fact, the familiar dandelion 'flower' is a composite of many small, individual flowers packed tightly together in a head known as a floret. Although pollinated by many animals making use of their nectar, dandelions in fact can set seed without pollination, creating many genetically identical propagules and creating all manner of taxonomic difficulties that are beyond the scope of this short article!

TWICE OVER

B Y THE START of June, one of Britain's many fine woodland and garden
birds is in full voice.

The poet Robert Browning celebrated the song of this magnificent bird in
the rhyme " *That's the wise thrush; he sings each song twice over, lest you should
think he never could recapture the first fine careless rapture!"*

Repetition of phrases within long and diverse mellifluous vocalisations is
indeed one of the distinctive features of the song of the common thrush (*Turdus
philomelos*), a bird also known as the song thrush for its melodious qualities.

The song thrush is a familiar British garden songbird. It is one of a
number of birds of the thrush family found in Britain, and also occurs right
across Europe. The song thrush has a catholic diet, feeding on a range of small
invertebrates as well as fruit. Thrushes are in the habit of hunting out snails
and taking them in their beaks to an 'anvil' – a crop of stone, a concrete step or
a fallen log – and repeatedly hammering them until the shell breaks, enabling
the bird to eat the soft body within. Shards of smashed shells give away the
locations of these anvil sites.

The song thrush is characterised by warm-brown plumage on the head, wings and back, with its cream-coloured breast covered in well-defined dark brown spots said to resemble the shape of upside-down hearts. It is not a big bird, with a wingspan of 33 to 36 centimetres. This is the same size as the closely related blackbird (*Turdus merula*) as well as two winter migrant thrushes that arrive from Scandinavia to overwinter in Britain: the redwing (*Turdus iliacus*) and the slightly larger fieldfare (*Turdus pilaris*). Song thrushes are potentially confused with the mistle thrush (*Turdus viscivorus*), though 'mistles' – so named for the fondness for mistletoe berries – are larger and more robustly built birds with a wingspan of 42-48 centimetres, a more greyish back, and with flecks on the chest rather than the neater spots of the song thrush.

Song thrushes can be seen in Britain all year round, favouring woodlands and hedgerows but also commonly in gardens. They start singing in early spring, in some years as early as January, often peaking when breeding commences in March or April and continuing into the early summer. During this time, thrushes may sing all day, though most particularly they do so early in the morning and often from high vantage points in trees and bushes to announce their presence to the world.

Browning was not the only author sufficiently enchanted to write about the song thrush. Thomas Hardy wrote the poem "*The darkling thrush*", capturing the invisibility of the bird in a copse yet revealed by its fluting song: "*At once a voice arose among, The bleak twigs overhead, In a full-hearted evensong, Of joy illimited; An aged thrush, frail, gaunt and small, In blast-beruffled plume, Had chosen thus to fling his soul, Upon the growing gloom*".

William Wordsworth too was smitten, with his own ode to this widespread and tuneful bird in his poem 'The Tables Turned': "*Hark, how blithe the throstle sings, And he is no mean preacher, Come forth into the light of things, Let Nature be your teacher*".

Thrushes have been trapped for food with records dating back over millennia, including an early reference in the Odyssey. In fact, hunting still continues around the Mediterranean, with thrush trapping using birdlime (an adhesive substance spread on branches or twigs: a practice that is technically illegal) still permitted and occurring in the Valencian region of Spain.

Song thrushes were also, at least up to the nineteenth century, kept in captivity as caged birds on account of their melodious song.

Today, I am simply happy to hear this wonderful bird in full voice in the wild in woodlands, gardens, bankside copses and hedgerows.

THE FRIENDLY
YELLOW PARASITE

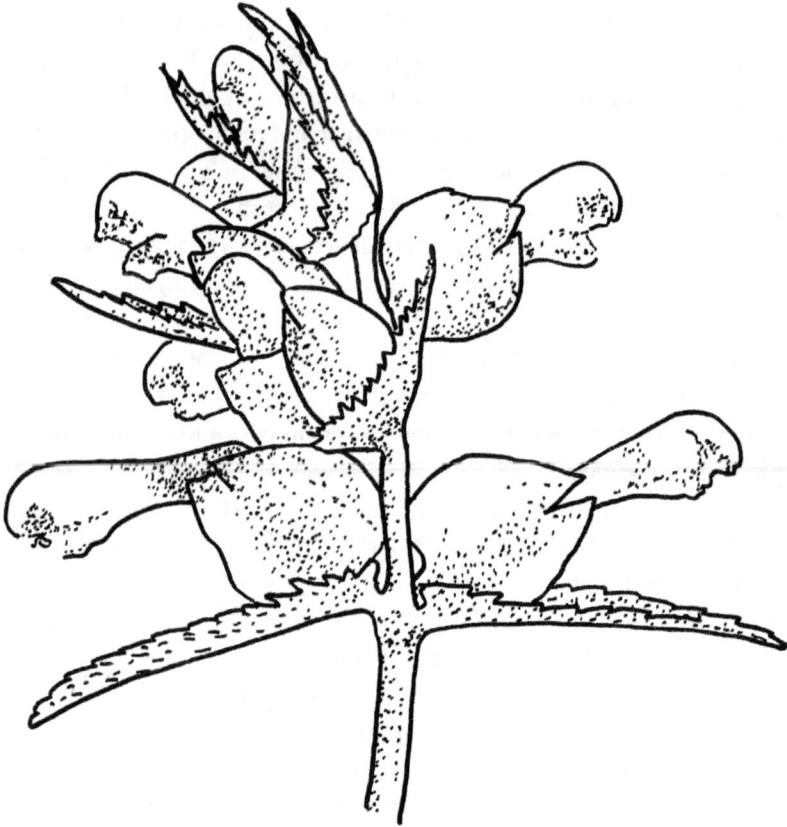

PARASITES GENERALLY HAVE a bad reputation. The reality, though, is that parasites are everywhere in nature, profiting from the productivity of host organisms.

It is reckoned that half of all animals on this planet are parasites. Nematode worms, for example, are the most numerous multicellular animals on Earth, accounting for about 80% of animal species globally in all environments. This includes within the bodies of other animals and plants, where many live parasitic lifestyles.

A few parasites cause disease. Many more live in mutual associations wherein harm is hard to ascertain. There is, in reality, a spectrum of associations between organisms ranging from the harmful to the beneficial.

The abundance of fungi, archaea, bacteria and other microorganisms in the rhizosphere (the immediate region of soil around plant roots) was once thought to be largely to the benefit of the microbes, until it was realised that not only do virtually all plants have these associations but that the plants release as much as half of their annual production of sugars to this microbial assemblage. In evolutionary terms, this apparent detriment to the plant's productivity could not be by accident. The reality is that the associated microbial ecosystem returns the favour to the plant by facilitating access to water and soil minerals, offering protection from pests and potential diseases, and providing a range of other benefits essential for the health of the host plant.

However, even parasites that can cause detriment to other species may, when viewed in the context of the wider ecosystem within which they are integral, serve beneficial functions. Some attack disease organisms or vectors of diseases, such as mosquitoes and some molluscs. Others weaken the dominance of other organisms, creating space for a greater diversity of less competitive species to prosper.

In fact, parasites generally benefit from their host's survival (unless the parasite occupies an 'intermediate host' that needs to be consumed by its final host). So, a well-evolved parasite may have little or no negative impact on the health of its host. This is said to be the case for tapeworms in humans.

Some plants too are parasitic. One parasitic plant common in grasslands deserves special mention: a hemi-parasitic annual plant known as yellow rattle (*Rhinanthus minor*). Yellow rattle is a common herb up to 45 centimetres (18 inches) tall with a yellow flower, occurring in grassland on varying soil types where it flowers from May and sometimes as late as September. This plant has a wide circumpolar distribution in the northern hemisphere across Europe, Russia, western Asia and northern North America. It has also been introduced to other parts of the world, including into Australia. Yellow rattle also goes by a range of other common names across Britain, including little yellow rattle, Rhinanthus, hay rattle, rattle basket and cockscomb.

Yellow rattle is referred to as a hemi-parasite as, though it can generate sustenance through photosynthesis, it also parasitises the roots of other plants, particularly grasses, drawing from them a substantial proportion of its nutrients. Far from damaging grasslands, yellow rattle thereby suppresses the growth of otherwise dominant grass species allowing a wide range of other wildflower species to compete and thrive, diversifying the sward.

The small, yellow tube-like flowers of the yellow rattle bloom in late spring or early summer. The flowers serve as valuable sources of nectar for a variety of insects, including bees and butterflies, that are also important as pollinators of other plant species, some of which are also predators of potential pest invertebrates. After the flowering season, the capsule of dry sepals (the calyx) fills with seeds that rattle when disturbed by walkers or the wind, giving the plant the second half of its common name. The small seeds tend to be dispersed by the wind, or else drop into the meadow sward near the parent plant.

Yellow rattle seeds remain in the soil throughout the winter months, requiring vernalisation (exposure to prolonged cold) to enable them to germinate the following spring. Yellow rattle seeds can be exploited as a food source by some animals, and the leaves are eaten by the larvae of two rare moth species including the grass rivulet (*Perizoma albulata*) the larvae of which feed on the ripening seeds of yellow rattle. Yellow rattle seeds have formerly been consumed by people, and the plant has also been used to make a yellow dye.

Nothing in nature is ever simple, all species meshing with others in complex ecosystems forged throughout millennia of evolution. And this is even – or perhaps especially – the case for parasites, which do not automatically deserve the bad reputations commonly ascribed to them!

LIVING DODGEMS

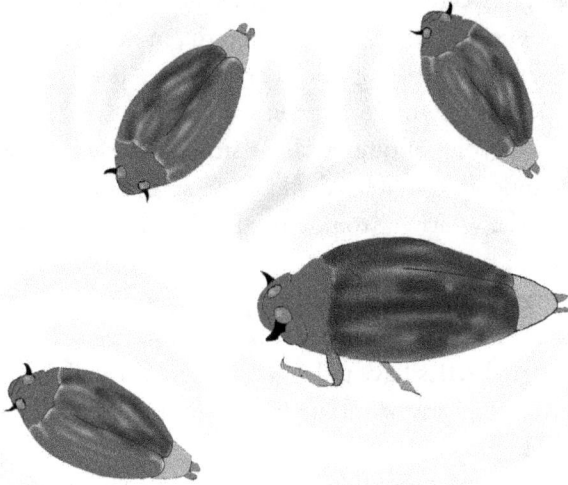

ONE OF THE most aptly named of aquatic insects is the whirligig beetle. Like so many frenzied glossy black dodgems, they can be spotted on the surface of pools and river margins from springtime through to the dying days of autumn. For the most part, they glide as a group with others of their kind, but they may also break out into a chaotic swarm whizzing around in erratic patterns.

Whilst a weaving mass of whirlygigs may appear as so many pea-sized black dodgems, miraculously they never collide with each other. For this reason, they are being studied amongst other reasons to inform the programming of robots to avoid collisions.

For those that remember demonstrations of Brownian motion in their school days, there is something familiar about the orderly chaos of the movements of these gatherings of whirlygigs cruising the surface film. Often, these beetles will assemble in suitable areas of the water's surface in placid groups, but they launch readily into their manic dance when threatened or vulnerable, particularly in open water. They can even dive and swim

underwater to evade predators, though whirlygigs are mainly animals
elegantly adapted to living in the surface film.

Another of the many remarkable adaptations of the whirligig beetle
is that it has four eyes. Insects have complex compound eyes comprising
clusters of ommatidia (individual light-sensitive units collectively comprising
the compound eye). Half of these ommatidia in each eye cluster located
on either side of the whirlygig's head are oriented downward below the
surface film, detecting what is happening below the water's surface. The
upper half of the group of ommatidia is situated above water level, sensing
what is happening above. This dual vision, side-to-side and above-and-
below, attunes the whirligig to potential food, predators and other aspects of
interest all around.

Whirlygigs, like many beetles, are predators, ready to pounce on small
creatures trapped in the surface film. Like pond skaters – other 'walkers on
water' – whirligig beetles have radar-like perception as they constantly sense
the finest of vibrations in the surface film, betraying prey, currents and would-
be predators alike.

Also like most beetles, whirlygigs can spread their wings and take to the
air. The hydrophobic (water-repelling) glossy back carapace armouring the
insect's back in fact comprises a pair of horny elytra, or keratinised forewings.
The pair of hindwings mainly lies tucked up dry and secure beneath the elytra
but can be spread rapidly. This enables the insect to take to the air as an
extreme avoidance of predators, or to migrate to new waters often for mating
thus maintaining genetic diversity. When the wings are folded, the whirligig
retains a bubble of air under the elytra enabling it to dive under the water
without notice. This captive bubble also acts as a supplementary gill, enabling
a whirligig beetle to remain underwater for extended periods.

The design of the whirligig beetle is so efficient that around 700 species
in the family Gyrinidae occur across the world, all of them very similar in
form with an ellipsoid body ranging between species from 3 to 18 millimetres
long. All are black, grey or dark brown, appearing shiny due to the smooth
and hydrophobic surface of their carapace. The antennae are short, plump
and oriented close to the water's surface, where they constantly sense fine
disturbances in the surface film. The front legs are short and adapted for
grabbing prey, whilst the rear legs are longer for efficient propulsion. 12 species
of whirligig beetle occur in British waters, ranging from 5 to 7 millimetres in
length.

Whirlygigs are social insects, using their radar-like senses to form sometimes tight clusters. The hungriest individuals tend to occupy the outer edges of these assemblages, giving them the benefit of quickest access to food but taking the greatest risk from predation. Under threat, the group can break into its manic dance to confuse would-be predators.

Whirlygig beetles lay eggs under the water's surface, typically on the surfaces of submerged water plants. Predatory larvae emerge from these eggs, growing on before pupating and then metamorphosing into surface-dwelling adult beetles.

You may well have seen groups of these black dots – dodgems of the surface film – careering across the surface of a pool or slacker margin of a river. If not, keep your eyes open for them from spring to autumn, as they are yet another of the many joyful waterside sights!

HIMALAYAN PERIL

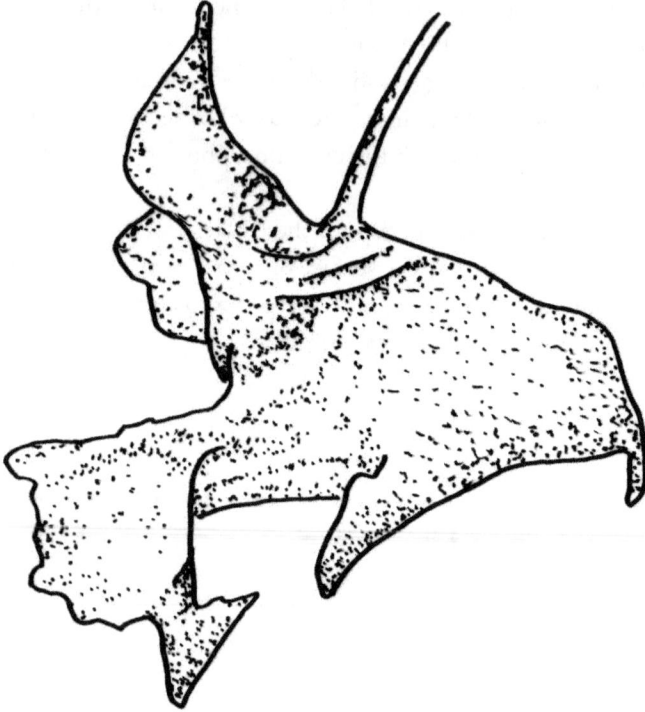

WHEN I WAS a small child in the early 1960s, tall, bright pink-flowered
Himalayan balsam (*Impatiens gladulifera*) plants made a spectacular
appearance by my then home river, Kent's River Medway. I loved them!
First introduced into Britain in 1839 by the horticultural trade, this attractive
annual plant is now widely naturalised across Britain and well known to most
of us. Its gaudy, pink 'Bobby's Helmet' flowers are beloved by bumblebees,
and its waxy aroma can be heady during the kind of long, hot summer days
that pervade childhood memories. And, of course, they have those spectacular
seed pods that, as they dry, 'explode' on contact, scattering seeds as far away
as four metres (or twelve feet in 'old money'). These plants are adapted, as
precisely as only nature can fashion, to their riparian niche.

But, to wax too long and lyrically about Himalayan balsam is to obscure
the ecological devastation that can result from this non-native plant species in

a British context, like so many other species released beyond the constraints
of the ecosystems with which they co-evolved. Himalayan balsam, along
with other problematic invasive plants such as giant hogweed (*Heracleum
mantegazzianum*), Australian swamp-stonecrop (*Crassula helmsii*) and
Japanese knotweed (*Fallopia japonica*), now occurs widely along British rivers,
thriving and in so doing resulting in a host of problems.

Though their flowers provide nectar for bumblebees in exchange for the
insect's pollination services, Himalayan balsam plants form tall, dense stands
in riverine landscapes that aggressively outcompete a diversity of native plants,
expunging them together with their associated wealth of dependent insect and
other wildlife. Worse still, these annual, shallow-rooted plants die back in
winter, exposing bare earth that is denuded of the tight root structure of native
plants. Soils consequently erode, destabilising riverbanks. Dislodged sediment
clogs submerged water plants and the pores of river gravels vital for small river
life, including the flush of oxygenated water essential for survival of the eggs of
gravel-spawning fishes such as trout, salmon, grayling, chub, dace and barbel.
Furthermore, eroding soils – lost as the primary capital of agriculture – carry
with them nutrient chemicals contributing to water quality problems, further
threatening river life and necessitating greater investment of energy, chemicals
and cash to treat water abstracted downstream for human uses.

Where plant species co-evolve in intimate connection with their grazers,
predators, parasites, competitors and pollinators, they play important
functional roles in time-hewn ecosystem processes and cycles. But, take those
genes, or genies, out of their metaphorical bottles, and they can run amok
without the checks and balances of naturally co-evolved grazers and predators,
with unforeseen and not infrequently deleterious consequences. Our common
and multi-beneficial riparian willow trees, for example, provide us and our
native ecosystems with a host of benefits, yet are a major cause of erosion and
other problems in the rather different types of rivers and wetland landscapes
found across Australia where these trees have become naturalised after
introduction.

We are getting better at controlling cavalier, and with hindsight
frankly reckless, release of non-native species. Legislation controlling the
introduction of live fishes includes schedules listing a number of potentially
problematic species, but also implicitly applying to any non-native species
capable of forming self-sustaining populations. We are far less assiduous about
controlling introductions of alien plants, despite a litany of 'horror stories'

about adverse and, largely, irreversible unintended negative consequences. Such is the power of, and vested interests in, the horticultural trade. Needless to say, I am an embarrassment in a garden centre when I start ranting about all this not only sanctioned but well-rewarded genetic pollution! (And don't even get me started about our continuing trade and widespread use of peat, destroying habitats and ecosystems that have taken millennia to form, liberating all that stored climate-active carbon, and robbing landscapes of their 'sponge effect' abating flood risk!)

My work takes me to the Middle Himalayas of India and Nepal. I see Himalayan balsam in the Indian Himalayas, but in modest stands co-mingling with a diversity of other native plants. Plant species with dense seeds resisting wash-out, and that shoot and mature rapidly as river flows subside, form the dominant annual vegetative cover across wide, boulder-strewn mountain river valleys scoured seasonally by violent monsoon spates. Acre after acre of *Cannabis sativa* are commonplace in these summer river valley bottoms, a species in its place elegantly adapted to that niche and supporting a diversity of native wildlife and traditional human uses. But that's a story for another day.

Back in Blighty, I'd encourage you to pull up any shallow-rooted Himalayan balsam plants that you see by the river, particularly before they flower and seed, to give our native wildlife a fair chance.

JULY

FLYING ANT DAY

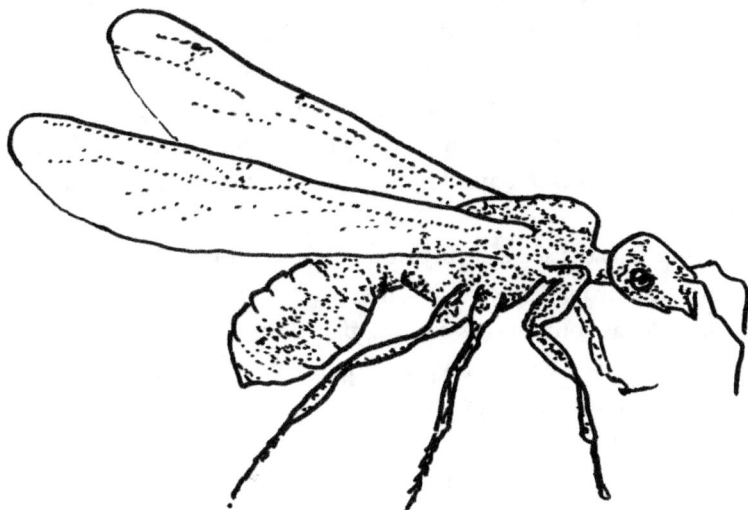

J ULY IS THE month when hordes of flying ants may suddenly appear, their emergence apparently synchronised over large areas. Out from cracks in patios, lawns and flower beds they emerge in their droves, often accumulating indoors.

For many, this plague of flying ants is a nuisance. It is, though, yet another of nature's underappreciated everyday miracles.

Ants are social insects closely related to wasps (both in the order Hymenoptera), with an estimated total of 22,000 species globally of which more than 13,800 have been classified by science. Around 65 native and introduced ant species are found across Britain. Some of these species are cosmopolitan: the black garden ant (*Lasius niger*) is one of the most widespread and is found across Europe and in some parts of North America, South America, Asia and Australasia. Other ant species are specialised in their adaptation to specific environments and lifestyles.

Ants are an ancient group of animals, the oldest ant fossils dating back around 100 million years ago in the mid-Cretaceous period. Ants have populated virtually every landmass on Earth, except in Antarctica and some scattered islands, and have adapted to a wide diversity of climates and food sources.

Colony size varies between species, from several dozen insects up to large nests holding hundreds of millions of individuals. Like wasps, colonies of most ant species comprise various castes. The majority are sterile, wingless 'worker' females. Some species have a 'soldier' caste, which is larger, stronger and generally armed with fierce mandibles (jaws). A small minority are winged, fertile males. Importantly, most ant colonies have one or more 'queens', which are large and fertile females with the role of pumping out eggs; once mated, a queen can stay fertilised for many years laying millions of eggs. Some queens lay thousands each day. The eggs are taken away and cared for by the workers.

So complex is the social structure and division of labour that large colonies are regarded as 'superorganisms', within which all individuals perform set roles as components of a singular unified entity. Lifespan varies with species and caste, workers typically living for between 4 and 12 months whilst queens can live up to 15 years.

Beyond their simple nuisance value, ant species in some countries are known to damage crops and to invade buildings. When I worked in Texas, the invasive fire ant (*Solenopsis invicta*), colonising from South America, was a particularly common pest with a painful bite.

However, look beyond these factors and ants bring us many benefits. Many societies across the world use ants as food. In Chinese traditional medicine, ants are consumed in powdered form or as extracts for their analgesic and anti-inflammatory properties. Ant products also serve as painkillers in Amazonia and as wound treatments in Africa. Ants also feature in cultural rituals, for example a rite of passage for young men of the Sateré-Mawé people in the Amazon involves placing the hand in a glove filled with the bullet ant (*Paraponera clavata*), which is notorious for its painful bite. Some ant species serve valuable roles as biological pest control agents.

Beyond human utility, ants are fed on by many other species, particularly birds and fish not to mention anteaters and a wide range of other mammals. The green woodpecker (*Picus viridis*), Britain's largest woodpecker species, subsists primarily on ants, which is why these birds are often sighted feeding from ant nests located in short turf such as in lawns, parks and other short-grass habitats.

Ants are also nature's great recyclers. They have been found to dominate waste management in tropical rainforests, where they are responsible for moving more than half of food resources from the rainforest floor. They thereby play vital roles in maintaining a healthy ecosystem. Ants therefore constitute 'ecosystem engineers', as their activities profoundly influence nutrient cycling, soil structure and the vitality of the whole ecosystem.

So why do ants take to the wing in huge numbers in a synchronised way, forming swarms that may be up to a mile long? This high degree of synchronisation is known as Flying Ant Day, typically occurring over a number of days in mid-July during hot weather. The phenomenon is explained by the mass emergence of new winged queen ants that take to the air to meet up with winged males and to travel to set up new colonies.

We humans often dismiss the small in favour of the gigantic. But, in many ways, Flying Ant Day is as dramatic, perhaps more so, and is certainly more ecologically significant than such spectacles as the iconic mass migration of wildebeest on the Masai Mara. In an increasingly beleaguered world that is seeing a cataclysmic collapse of its hugely important insect fauna, we should learn to better appreciate our smallest partners.

UPSIDE-DOWN TREES

MANY AMONGST US may recall the infamous British drought of 1976. Low rainfall throughout the prior winter followed by hot and arid conditions spanning months reduced the landscape to buff-hued savannah, crops to stunted stands and rivers to mere trickles. The 'Dunkirk spirit' was very much in evidence as we gathered around standpipes and hoarded every drop of precious water. Many followed the government advice to "*Save water; bath with a friend*"; I certainly did, but then it was the 1970s and I was a free-wheeling student!

But the mighty oaks and other larger standard trees endured, or so we thought. What was to follow in the succeeding years though was the slow and sad demise of many venerable landmark trees. The following dry summer of 1977 certainly did not help matters. What we later came to appreciate was that, although apparently thriving, these icons in the landscape were already dying, but doing so in a slow and dignified manner. The sap and moisture stored in the heartwood of the trunk eked out another season or two of leaves unfurling and acorns maturing, though perhaps as a last gasp to pass on genes to following generations. Damage had been done, generally irreversibly, to the minute rootlets and their attendant microbial communities deep down and hidden below the desiccated soil surface.

I sometimes think of rivers as 'upside-down trees', and I worry.

Why so? The large main 'trunks' of rivers are resilient to a diversity of pressures arising across the wide catchments that feed them. The sheer volume of their 'heartwood' buffers perturbations arising from disparate, fragmented land use changes and other developments, differential rainfall across the catchment landscape, and the attentions of avian and other predators. But this is not so for the smaller headwaters and tributaries, which are the metaphorical but also in many ways quite literal roots upon which the 'trunks' of larger downstream river reaches depend.

Taking a walk through arable landscapes after heavy rainfall may reveal moist flushes cutting across tilled soil. In natural conditions, these damp runnels may well have been ephemeral headwaters. Ditches running thick with eroded topsoil, bearing away this fast-declining primary resource and with it a cocktail of agrochemicals, hardly bodes well for the health of downstream reaches. In grazing landscapes, headwaters fare little better; trampled, manured and largely forgotten other than as moist depressions as groundwater breaks the surface after heavy seasonal rains.

The story in urban areas is often far worse. Streams that once ran clear and fresh have become progressively constricted by built development and infrastructure, all too often now frequently littered and contaminated into habitat-sparse drainage conduits frequently darkened and oiled by run-off and other effluent. These now urbanised streams may have historically served as valued sources of water, grazing and power as foundational resources for earlier settlements, the names of which not infrequently reflect watery underpinnings that are now all too often forgotten, decimated and desiccated.

Land is made increasingly impermeable around these precious watery 'roots' – by paving in urban places and by soil compaction in farmed land – exacerbating erosive flood peaks whilst preventing percolation into the groundwater that smooths flows throughout drier seasons.

Though the fate of these headwaters may be unwelcomingly familiar, there is little or no recognition of the gravity of threat this poses for the 'trees' of downstream river systems. These small and too-often discounted 'rootlet' streams are the sources of fresh flows and of invertebrate and other biodiversity that also serves as a primary food source for downstream ecosystems. The multiple, heterogeneous headwaters are the spawning and nursery habitats to which fish and other wildlife migrate to complete their life cycles. Cumulatively, they comprise the wellsprings of life – figuratively and literally – of the whole river system, including all the benefits that in confers upon humanity.

No runnel is too small to matter. We knew as children, most of us living close to apparently inconsequential brooks rather than imposing lower rivers, that each was a place of wonder and mystery, sticklebacks and minnows, caddis larvae and dragonflies, and a place of infinite enjoyment to play 'Pooh sticks' or otherwise find healthy entertainment.

We knew then the everyday miracles within those small watery worlds. We need to rediscover and act upon that reality, protecting and restoring the life-giving roots of these 'upside-down trees' before our rivers wither away in a protracted and dignified decline like those now fondly remembered veteran oaks of the late 1970s.

WORMS IN FOOTBALL JERSEYS

A NOTHER OF MY many favourite childhood memories of summertime on riparian meadows is of 'Worms in football jerseys'. These are the vivid yellow-and-black annular-banded caterpillars of the cinnabar moth (*Tyria jacobaeae*), found feeding on the heads of species of ragwort (*Senecio* species).

As we know from wasps and hornets, yellow and black stripes are one of nature's codes for "*Predators beware!*" Many animals with this striped pattern – insects, frogs, sea slugs, fishes amongst others – pack a sting or contain toxins or distasteful chemicals. In common with many such grazing animals, the conspicuous caterpillars of the cinnabar moth not only graze brazenly by day but also accumulate toxic and noxious chemicals from the plants they consume.

Cinnabar moth eggs may be laid on certain other plants, including groundsel (*Senecio vulgaris*), but larger ragwort species are favoured food plants from which newly hatched larvae start to absorb toxic and bitter-tasting alkaloid substances as they feed. This makes them unpalatable to most other animals. But cinnabar moth caterpillars are not entirely vegan; when they deplete their food plants, it is not unknown for them to turn cannibal.

Adult cinnabar moths have long antennae and a black body colour, day-flying moths that are commonly seen on the wing in broad daylight in May and June. The upper surfaces of the forewings are iridescent black flecked with vermillion patches, and the upper surfaces of the hindwings are also prominently vermillion. This gaudy colour gives the moth its common name, cinnabar being the bright sulphide ore from which the highly toxic metal mercury is extracted.

Whilst the contrasting bright colours of larvae and adult cinnabar moths act as warning signs, certain animals favour feeding on caterpillars armed with hairs, poisons and other deterrents. Amongst these is the common cuckoo (*Cuculus canorus*).

'Worms in football jerseys' will be with us from June to August, feeding conspicuously by day on ragworts whilst advertising their warning credentials, before pupating in the soil. The adult, day-flying moths emerge typically between May and July.

The cinnabar moth is one of many species of day-flying moths found in Britain. Others include the tiger moth (*Arctia caja*), burnet moth (several species of *Zygaena*), hummingbird hawk moth (*Macroglossum stellatarum*) and the bee hawk moth (two species of *Hemaris*). However, I got into all sorts of trouble trying to explain this to friends in France.

The French word for 'moth' is 'papillon de nuit' (literally 'butterfly of the night'). One fine day in the South of France, some French friends asked what insects were feeding on their flowers (they were 'Sphinx', one of the French terms for the hummingbird hawk moth.) I explained these insects were "*papillons de nuit qui volent pendant la journée*" (moths that fly during the day). This literally translates as "*butterflies of the night that fly during the day*").

"*Mais non! Ils sont papillons!*" ("*No, they are butterflies!*")

I am sure that there is a French scientific term for 'day-flying moth', but I have long since given up trying to explain the concept to lay Francophones!

The cinnabar moth naturally occurs throughout Europe and through western and central Asia. As the caterpillars are so voracious, often clearing large areas of ragwort plants, they can serve as successful biocontrol agents as ragwort can be problematic for livestock owing to its toxicity even when dried out in hay. It is for biocontrol purposes that cinnabar moths have now been introduced into New Zealand, Australia and North America.

The contrasting technicolour cinnabar moth caterpillars and adults add yet more hues and textures to the rich tapestry of mid-summer meadows, also favouring sandy heaths and other dry terrain where ragwort abounds.

ASHEN

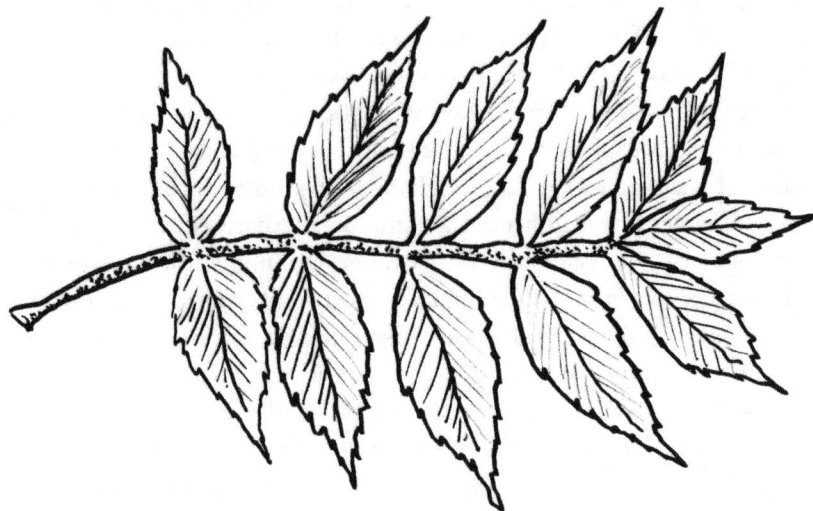

THE ASH TREE (*Fraxinus excelsior*) is one of the most familiar, characteristic, widespread and best loved trees found across the British Isles and northern continental Europe. These are tall and graceful trees, a fully-grown ash as tall as 35 metres (115 feet), often found growing together and forming a domed canopy. The bark of the ash is a characteristic silvery-grey when young, fading to pale brown with fissures as the tree ages. The overwintering twigs of this deciduous tree are smooth, slightly flattened, and have black, velvety leaf buds arranged opposite each other.

When the spring arrives, the leaf buds open to produce pinnate leaves comprising, generally, 3-6 pairs of pale green, oval and opposite leaflets with one terminal leaflet, the whole pinnate leaf up to 40 centimetres (about 16 inches) long. The leaves fan out forming a green canopy that, when their work is done in late autumn, fall when still green.

Another interesting feature of the ash is that it is dioecious, male and female flowers typically growing on different trees although some trees can have male and female flowers on different branches. Both male and female flowers are purple, emerging as spiked clusters from the stem before the leaves unfurl in spring. Ash flowers are wind-pollinated and, once pollinated, female flowers develop into conspicuous winged fruits, or 'keys'. The keys fall from the trees in late summer and autumn, dispersed by the wind and by the actions of birds and mammals.

Much more could be written about the fascinating biology and cultural associations of this familiar tree, but more needs to said about a scourge amongst British ash that threatens its very survival.

Ash dieback disease, also known as 'chalara', was first recognised in Britain in the 2012, though it may have been spreading undetected since before that time. It is caused by the fungus *Hymenoscyphus fraxineus* (formerly known as *Chalara fraxineus* hence the common alternative name of the disease) originating in Asia. In its native range, the fungus affects Manchurian ash (*Fraxinus mandshurica*) and Chinese ash (*Fraxinus chinensis*), causing these trees little harm. However, the disease first appeared in Europe around the early 1990s. Our native ash species has little or no resistance.

Ash dieback can affect European ash trees of all ages, younger trees generally succumbing the quickest though all trees are vulnerable. Affected trees display any of a range of symptoms, often in combination, some of which include the development of dark patches on the leaves in summer, early shedding of leaves or die-back of shoots, and formation of lesions on the branches or trunk. The fungus overwinters in leaf litter on the ground, particularly on ash leaf stalks, producing small white fruiting bodies between July and October which release spores into the surrounding atmosphere. These spores can blow up to tens of miles away.

Ash dieback is projected to kill around 80% of ash trees across the UK, changing the landscape permanently. The loss of ash trees also threatens many species reliant on them as a food plant, including many moths and other insects. It also depletes the availability of nesting and nest-building materials, reduces the cycling of carbon and other substances, removes wind breaks, and affects ecosystems and landscape-scale functions in many other ways.

Once infected by ash dieback, larger ash trees tend to then get invaded by honey fungus. The honey fungus spreads throughout the tree, breaking down its internal structure, and can result in heavy branches suddenly crashing down at great risk to people, animals and infrastructure. Infected trees require urgent attention, with mass felling of stands of ash often required once the disease takes hold. The cumulative implications of the loss of ash trees and the management of infected trees runs into billions of pounds.

This is a deadly pandemic, and already the spores are so widely dispersed that we are beyond the hope of biosecurity preventing further spread. We just have to wait to see the catastrophic ramifications as the disease spreads. There is already massive mortality of ash trees in the south and east of Britain, particularly in ash-dominated woodlands where the trees are in closest proximity, with the disease already evident throughout the country and gaining pace.

Is there any hope? Initial findings suggest that some trees may be tolerant to ash dieback, and these are being propagated with a view to replacing older hedge and standard trees. However, this may take decades.

Ash trees, currently abundant and charismatic in our landscapes, are at great risk. Once you take note of them, you suddenly wake up to how widespread they are. Ash dieback may not be a story with a happy ending, at least in short or medium terms. It amplifies the importance of future sound environmental practice and biosecurity to prevent the transboundary spread of novel diseases, and why it matters that we better safeguard the resilience of remaining components of our ecosystems against the inevitable loss of many ash trees.

THE HUM OF
SUMMER MOTHS

I T IS AT this time of year that I tend to get phone calls, emails and other
messages that some weird creature or other has made an appearance in
someone's garden or around their pot plants. This is the early summer season
of plenty – small mammals, exotic-looking moths, vivid or furry caterpillars,
colourful birds, etc. – but one creature in particular dominates these calls.

Typical calls include "*I thought I saw a hummingbird in my flower
bed!*" or "*Some odd bee-type creature was hovering near my window box!*"
Well, dear reader, you may just have seen a hummingbird, but this was not
(necessarily) of the feathered kind!

It is at this time of year that the hummingbird hawk moth
(*Macroglossum stellatarum*) tends to appear. The insect is so named as it
feeds on the wing very much like, and closely resembling, a hummingbird.
Hummingbird hawk moths feed on the nectar of tube-shaped flowers. To
access this nectar, they are armed with a very long proboscis (the proboscis is

25–28 millimetres or 0.98–1.10 inches long compared to the insect's wingspan of 40–45 millimetres or 1.6–1.8 inches). The insect hovers in the air with rapid wingbeats as it inserts its proboscis down into the flower tube to reach the nectaries (specialised nectar-producing structures of the flower). Sometimes, in quiet surroundings, the hum of the hovering moth is audible.

Hummingbird hawk moths are widely distributed across Eurasia from Portugal in the west to Japan in the east. However, they mainly breed in the warmer climates of southern Europe, North Africa and eastwards. Two or more broods are produced each year and, in some warmer regions, breeding occurring throughout the year. In Spain, this moth may produce as many as three generations in a year.

Hummingbird hawk moths fly strongly, these insects dispersing widely throughout the summer and populating many regions northwards though rarely surviving winters in latitudes north of the Alps in Europe or the Caucasus in Russia. It is moths migrating northwards, possibly having travelled hundreds of miles, that begin to arrive in Britain sometimes in significant numbers around July.

This is a moth that flies during the day. In fact, contrary to common assumptions, there are many British moth species that fly during the day. Hummingbird hawk moths favour hunting for nectar in bright sunshine when flowers are at their most visible and open, though they will also be seen on the wing at dusk and dawn. They can even fly in the rain, which is unusual amongst other moths and butterflies. Hummingbird hawk moths also have highly developed colour vision and an ability to learn colours, helping them locate suitable flowers as food sources as the high energetic costs of hovering flight require constant fuelling.

As I mentioned previously when writing about the cinnabar moth, discussion with people in France about day-flying moth can be frustrating! As many readers will know, the French word for 'moth' is 'papillon de nuit', literally meaning 'butterfly of the night'. As I noted before, I eventually saw the futility of trying the explain in French the concept of a 'day-flying moth', turning my attention instead to some nicely aromatic red wine!

Hummingbird hawk moths have in the past been recognised as a lucky omen. In particular, a swarm of these moths was seen on their migratory journey flying northwards across the English Channel on D-Day, 6th June 1944, the day of the Normandy landings by allied forces in the Second World War.

Whether lucky or not, the arrival of these spectacular moths is certainly a harbinger of the arrival of high summer, and so doubly to be welcomed!

AUGUST

BRANDY BOTTLE TIME

I N THE DROWSY days of summer, the pace of the river slows and formerly fresh vegetation begins to look tired. Amongst the often now dusty lily leaves in the margins of lowland rivers, green 'brandy bottles' poke their necks out of the water.

The yellow water lily (*Nuphar lutea*) is a common plant of still or slow-moving water, growing in lowland rivers, ponds, lakes, canals and ditches. This lily is also known at this time of year as the 'brandy-bottle', so-called after the shape of the seed pods peeking their rotund forms through the water's surface but also as the flower's aroma is similar to stale alcohol. The yellow water lily is very widely native across northern temperate and some subtropical regions both sides of the Atlantic Ocean, in Europe, north-west Africa, western Asia, North America and even down into Cuba.

Across this broad range, this lily goes by a huge diversity of local names, many in the languages of the places in which it occurs. The name 'beaver lily', 'beaver more' and 'beaver root' derive from the plant often thriving in the stilled water of beaver ponds. Just a few of the other English common names are bobber, bonnets, bullhead lily, can-dock, cow lily, dog lily, ducks, flatterdock, frog lily, globe lily, gold watch, hog lily, holy-trinity lily, horse lily, kelp, large yellow pond lily, lis d'eau jaune, marsh collaid, mooseroot,

mulefoot, mulefoot bonnet, mulefoot lily, muleshoe, nenuphar jaune, pied de
cheval, pond poppy, spatterdock, splatterdock, three coloured lily, toad lily,
tuckahoe, tuckey, tucky lily, water collard, wokas, yellow lanterns, and yellow
pond lily. Clearly a plant with broad appeal!

Many people will also recognise the plant as 'cabbages', colloquially
named after the appearance of the submerged leaves occurring year-round.
These submerged 'cabbage' leaves are particularly noticeable in clearer water
before the plant pushes up stalks as long as 3-5 metres throughout the spring
and summer, from with unfurl large, floating lily pad leaves that are up to 40
centimetres (around one-and-one-third feet) across.

It is in the late spring and early summer, from June to September, that
the long flower stalks of the yellow water lily extend and float to the surface.
Terminal buds open into solitary (one per stalk) yellow, cupped flowers borne
just above the water's surface.

Sometimes after major floods, you may also see large green rhizomes –
submerged stems usually unseen as they anchor the plant to the bed – ripped
out by spate currents and scattered across floodplains. Mostly, yellow water
lilies spread from these rhizomes in the bed of the water body, extending out
and pushing up new shoots. However, the 'brandy bottle' seed pods also
burst to release as many as 400 seeds – the common names 'spadderdock',
'splatterdock' or spatterdock' come from the spattering of seeds when the fruit
bursts – that disperse in the water before sinking. It may take seedlings up to
three years to flower.

The rhizomes of the yellow water lily, its submerged 'cabbage' leaves and
the forest of tall stems of floating leaves and flower stalks provide important
habitat harbouring invertebrates, amphibians, reptiles such as small turtles
in the countries in which they occur, but also resting places for grass snakes.
Various species of fish too make use of the physical habitat provided by lily
vegetation, which also supports a wealth of invertebrate life upon which fishes
of all life stages feed. Many larger animals may also graze on the stems, roots
and leaves.

Humans too have made use of yellow water lilies since prehistory.
Remnants of the plant's tubers and seeds have been discovered in artefacts
and remains dating back to Early Neolithic times (ᶜ10,000 years BCE). The
thick rhizomes have been gathered in more recent times for slicing, drying and
grinding into meal or flour. Heated seeds are said to swell like popcorn and
can reportedly be consumed as a crunchy snack.

In ancient Greece, Aristotle and Diodorus Siculus noted that the yellow water lily has distinct medicinal properties. Medicinal uses are still suggested for this plant in current times, including uses as an anaphrodisiac, anodyne, antiscrophulatic, antispasmodic, astringent, cardiotonic, demulcent, hypotensive, sedative and vasoconstrictor. Some of its chemical compounds are showing promise for their anti-inflammatory, antifungal and antibacterial actions. Recent research suggests that the yellow water lily may have potential for treatment of cancer and MRSA (a problematic antibiotic-resistant strain of bacteria), as well as Alzheimer's, Huntington's and Parkinson's diseases.

We are surrounded by nature's riches of broad ecological, cultural, medicinal, gastronomic, ornamental and other importance. And this is true even in the murky ditches, pools and streams in which these robust water plants thrive, but that we may too readily dismiss!

A SOUP OF FLEAS AND FISH

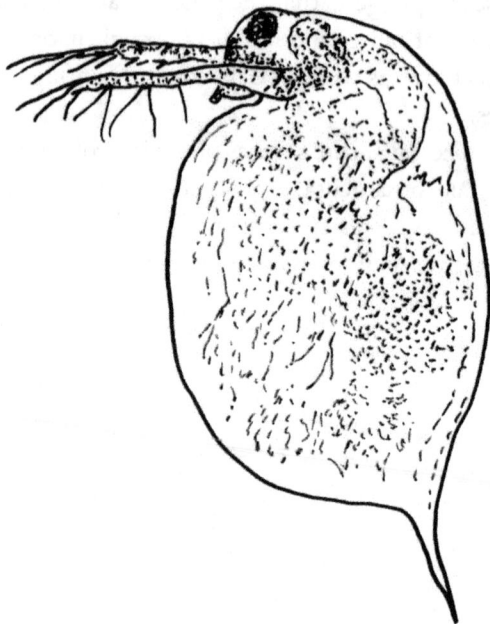

S OME RIVERS AND ponds have clear water. Other don't.
Some have waters muddied to varying degrees by loads of suspended sediment. Rivers, in particular, are affected by their underlying geology and upstream human and other activities.

The waters of many slower rivers, canals, lake and ponds can turn into a turbid green or brownish soup due to suspension of microscopic algae (known as phytoplankton), particularly in warmer and brighter weather and where they are enriched by nutrient chemicals.

Yet the waters of some pools and languid river can be clear, or else can recover their clarify over time after an algal bloom. Why could this be?

Looking into the margins of clear-water pools, you may be able to see some of the culprits. Peering closer, particularly around the stems of emergent reeds and other vegetation, you may see the water seething with small, erratically moving dots, each of them a millimetre or less in diameter. Amongst these are cladocerans, ostracods, copepods, rotifers and other exotic creatures. We need not fret about these longer names and their fascinating and widely differing forms and life histories, simply recognising them by the familiar name of 'water fleas'. Water fleas suspended in the water column are near-microscopic animals that feed by grazing on planktonic algae. (Water fleas, along with a range of insect larvae and other small animals suspended in the water column, collectively comprise the 'zooplankton'.)

Where zooplanktonic grazing animals are scarce, suspended algae (the phytoplankton) can prosper in nutrient-rich waters forming a turbid soup, or bloom. This is particularly so during warmer months and brighter weather. As numbers of water fleas increase and feast on the algae, they clear the water. A nice balance is maintained.

However, fish influence this equilibrium.

Some species of river and pond fish, such as rudd and roach, feast on the water fleas. High densities of zooplankton-eating fish can reduce the population of water fleas substantially, consequently enabling suspended algae in a slow river or pool to proliferate and once again turn the water into an algal soup.

Conversely, where numbers of zooplankton-eating fish are low, or where zooplankton is shielded in stands of larger water plants, the water flea population may thrive, in turn maintaining clear water conditions.

And this is where yet more fish come to play.

High populations of predatory fish, such as perch and pike, can suppress the population of the types of fish that feed on water fleas, thereby allowing water fleas to proliferate and maintain water clarity. The extra light penetration can encourage growth of submerged, rooted water plants. A rich growth of submerged water plants provides ideal ambush cover for the predatory fish, as well as directly absorbing dissolved nutrients depriving phytoplankton, reinforcing the clear-water balance.

Conversely, loss of rooted vegetation reduces the success rate of predatory fish, allowing zooplankton-eating fish to increase in numbers in turn suppressing water flea populations and so enabling the algae to bloom creating soupy, turbid waters. The opacity of these algal-rich waters may also decrease light penetration, suppressing coverage of rooted plants on the bed of the water body.

A bit confusing, granted, but think of it as two regimes: A cloudy-water regime lacking water fleas mainly due to predation by fish, and a clear-water regime maintained by thriving water fleas!

Then, of course, we throw in other fish species whose feeding habitats entail grubbing up the bed of the river or lake, for example common carp and common bream. These truffling feeding habits – a bit like pigs in overstocked fields – uproot submerged plants and resuspend sediment along with absorbed nutrients, creating a whole different type of muddy suspension in the water!

What happens under the surface influencing water clarity is really quite fascinatingly intricate. That's something to think about when you next walk by a pool or river, or look over a bridge, and reflect on the clarity of the water or the lack of it. There is really quite a lot going on down there!

LUNACY

T HE TERM 'LUNACY' was coined in the 1540s, describing intermittent
periods of insanity believed to be triggered by lunar cycle.

What's that got to do with river and aquatic life, you might ask? Quite
a lot, actually, from planetary scale right down to minute facets of animal
behaviour.

People throughout generations have noted associations between the
weather and lunar phases. The moon may be just under a quarter-of-a-
million miles (over a third-of-million kilometres) away from Planet Earth.
But, though distant, it is a substantial piece of rock, weighing in at roughly
one-eighth the mass of our planet. Its gravitational pull is consequently far
from insignificant. This manifests, for example, in the twice-daily bulge in
the sea that we experience as the tides. For marine and estuarine life, and the
organisms that transition through them into fresh waters or onto land, this

influence is profound.

This impact of the moon's erratic orbit on water systems is mirrored largely unseen in its tidal effect above the land and water surface on the planetary atmosphere. However, though not visible, the influence of lunar gravity on the Earth's climate and weather patterns are felt far more directly. Atmospheric tides cause energy flows between atmospheric layers, changing atmospheric pressure that, in turn, affects the amount of moisture that the air can carry with local implications for rainfall patterns. Lower air pressure is linked to erratic, wetter weather, and higher pressure creates drier, calmer conditions.

Weather patterns are also substantially influenced by ocean currents. The Gulf Stream, for example, brings moist, warm air north-eastwards across the north Atlantic, a major contributory factor to the British Isles being far warmer and better watered than would otherwise be the case at this latitude.

As oceanic flows change, cooler currents bring colder, drier weather. Globally, we see regular cycles of El Niño and El Niña. Under El Niño conditions, trade winds pile warm surface water near the west coast of South America, suppressing the normal upwelling of cold, nutrient-rich water that generates massive productivity. This lunar-driven southern hemisphere cycle, half a world away from us, exerts profound impacts on weather patterns at fully global scale. There is also a lunar cycle observable in the extent of polar ice. Even the land surface reacts to the lunar pull, deformation and bulges of the Earth's crust triggering volcanic activity and earthquakes.

The moon's diverse influences on planetary cycles significantly influences all living things. In fact, there have been suggestions that the stabilising effect of the moon's gravity on the Earth has been a significant contributor to the stability of the climate, in turn making conditions more possible for the emergence of life.

Lunar cycles trigger changes in animal behaviours, profoundly in coastal organisms but also inshore. Many migratory animals, including crabs, salmon and sea turtles, use the moon's position to navigate over long journeys. Some predators, such as owls and wolves, become more active during the full moon, in part as brighter moonlight makes it easier for them to locate prey. Prey animals, such as mice and rabbits, tend to become more active during the new moon, perhaps as they are less visible to predators during darker nights. The breeding of many animals – sea otters, fish, crabs, corals and others – is also known to be triggered by lunar cycles. The mechanisms by which lunar cycles affect animal behaviour are far from well understood. The intensity of moonlight plays only a contributory role, with the moon's gravitational pull and electromagnetic radiation thought to exert more propound stimuli. What is certain is that lunar rhythms, pre-existing the genesis of living organisms here on our home planet by billions of years, are integrally embedded in the cycles of life on Earth, including the atmospheric, tidal, weather and organisms of all types, governing how they go about the daily challenge of living.

There is also evidence that humans are affected by lunar cycles. There is a stronger likelihood that people are born during the time of the full moon. Mood swings are also reported as synchronised to the full moon. Also, sleep disturbance, which I can vouch for through my own lifelong direct experience regardless of whether there is heavy cloud cover blocking out moonlight. It may be that these effects are subtle and hard to discern in the general population, also masked by our addictions to television, tablets, phone and other screens and urban lighting, but also as people seem to be differentially sensitive.

In my own self-confessed lunacy, I am not alone, with other sensitive humans but also many or most other living creatures responding in diverse ways to the cycles of our constant companion satellite.

BEWARE OF THE
TIGERS!

A RIVER OR pond is a hazardous place to be if you are small fish, insect,
worm or pretty much any other animal. It is a 'dog-eat-dog' world out
there, with predatory birds, bugs, beetles, amphibians, fish, carnivorous plants
and many more organisms besides.

One of the more fearsome in our pools and rivers is the water tiger.

The water tiger in our temperate waters is no aquatic mammal. Nor is
it a fish, though the mahseer fishes of tropical and subtropical South and East
Asia rivers are top predators known colloquially as 'tigers of the river'. Our
domestic tigers are aquatic larvae of water beetles in the family Dytiscidae.

There are some 4,000 or so species of dytiscid beetles. Dytiscids are
found in virtually every freshwater habitat and many brackish ones around the
world, though a few live in leaf litter. They are mainly larger beetles, ranging

from between 1 and 2.5 centimetres (0.4–1.0 inches) long as adults, though some are almost twice this size.

Whilst the adult beetles are predatory, it is their aquatic larvae that attract the common name 'water tigers' due to their voracious appetites. The larval water tigers are generally yellow or brown in colour and can be relatively large, varying by species from approximately 1 to 5 centimetres (a half-inch to two inches) from the dorsoventrally flattened head to the end of the body. The body of the water tiger tapers towards a pair of modified, terminal spiracles, enabling these larvae to draw in air from the water's surface. Adult dytiscids also breath in this way, suspended below the surface to exchange gases before diving down into deeper water to hunt or to evade their predators.

To hunt, water tiger larvae hang motionless in vegetation using their six legs, waiting for potential prey to venture close. To capture and immobilise their prey, water tigers have a pair of short but sharp mandibles (robust mouthparts), one either side of the flattened head. Once a suitable prey animal approaches sufficiently closely, the water tiger lunges to trap the unfortunate organism between its front legs whilst biting down with its sharp mandibles and simultaneously delivering digestive enzymes. The liquefied contents of the prey are sucked in by the water tiger using a specialised organ known as a hydraulic pump, located in the head of the larvae and comprising a series of muscles and chambers. These muscles are contracted to create a vacuum in the chambers, drawing the contents of the prey's body into the mouth. This adaptation, characteristic of the dytiscids, enables larvae to suck up the contents of prey that is much larger than its own head.

A further feature of the hydraulic pump system is that it sucks up air, helping the larvae to move underwater. Air held in the largest of the three chambers – the reservoir chamber – can also be used to enable the water tiger to breathe underwater or to move around.

Where larger fish are present, they can predate on both the beetles and their larvae, suppressing the insect population. However, in densely vegetated margins and in pools where fish and their fry are smaller and sparse, the tables turn. Small fish species and the fry of larger ones, as well as amphibian larvae and many types of invertebrate fall foul of those ever-eager, fearsome and sharp mandibles.

Maturing dytiscid larvae crawl from the water, burying themselves in adjacent soft, wet mud where the form pupae. After around a week, or sometimes more, adult beetles emerge from the mud.

Like most beetles, the adult insect can fly. This enables them to colonise new water bodies. The rear pair of wings adapted for flying are folded beneath the elytra, which are a hardened front pair of wings forming a robust covering over the rear wings and forming the carapace of the adult insect.

Water tigers are both predator and prey, yet another of the endlessly fascinating roster of players within the complex ecosystems of the watery realm, playing crucial roles in maintaining flows of nutrients and energy.

Fascinating to watch, but do keep them well clear of any tadpoles and small fish that you may be keeping as pets!!

THE CARNIVORE HIDING IN THE BOG

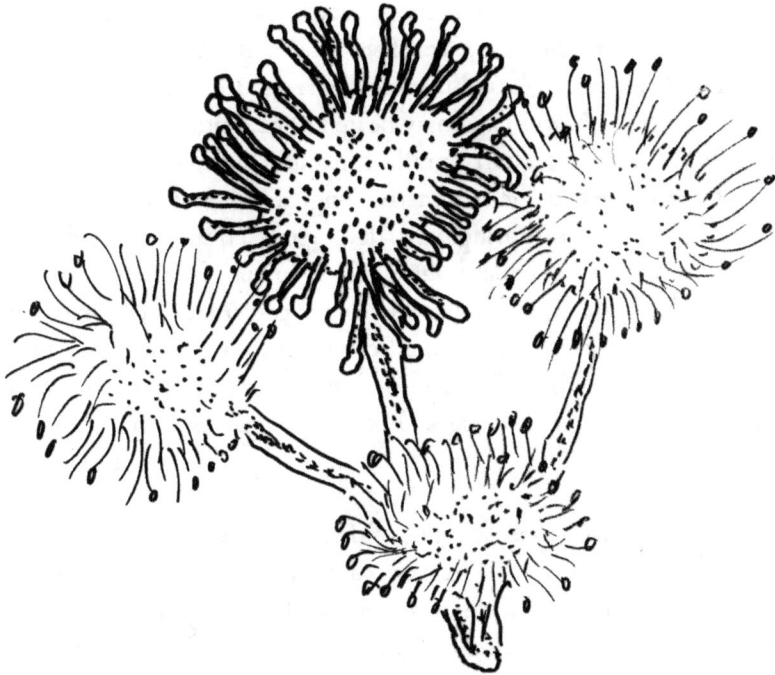

AKE CARE WHEN you go into the bog; there may be a carnivore lurking there!

Low-budget, mainly American, black-and-white horror movies featuring carnivorous plants were a staple of late-night Friday and Saturday television back in the 1960s. But we have more than a few carnivorous plants lurking right here in Britain.

Mainly, these are plants of wet peaty habitats, their carnivorous habits serving to obtain the nutrients – particularly nitrogen and phosphorus – that they can't obtain from the poor soils and waters on and in which they grow. Consequently, these plants are to be found mainly in the south-west, west and north of the British Isles, rather than in the more fertile lowlands across much of central and eastern lowland Britain. But, make no mistake, where they occur, they are hungry for animal food!

The most common and widespread of Britain's carnivorous plants is the round-leaved sundew (*Drosera rotundifolia*), also known as the common sundew. Other local names include dew plant, eyebright, moor-grass, red rot, rosa solis, youthwort, and also lustwort reflecting one of the plant's traditional uses as an aphrodisiac.

The round-leaved sundew is one of around 150 sundew species found in both temperate and tropical parts of the world. As the Latin name *Drosera rotundifolia* suggests, this species has rounded, spoon-shaped leaves that are reddish-green and may be up to one centimetre across. These rounded leaves are held on horizontally-spreading, hairy leaf stalks that may be between one and five centimetres long. The leaves are covered with sticky, red-tipped, gland-bearing hairs, developed to trap small insects. The round-leaved sundew has what is known as a 'circumpolar boreo-temperate' distribution, basically meaning that it occurs in cooler latitudes across the arctic/temperate interface. It is found from northern parts of North America and much of Canada, throughout much of Europe as well as parts of Turkey, the Caucasus region, the Kamchatka Peninsula, across Siberia and Japan, and in southern parts of Korea. Populations can also be found on the island of New Guinea.

The round-leaved sundew is one of three sundew species found across Europe, including in Britain. These two other British and European species are oblong-leaved sundew (*Drosera anglica*) and *Drosera intermedia*. The oblong-leaved sundew is distinguished by narrower leaves and long flowering stems, though this plant is extinct in much of England but still locally common in western Scotland. *Drosera intermedia* has small leaves that are narrowed into the stalks, intermediate is shape (as indicated by the specific name) to those of the round-leaved sundew and *Drosera anglica*, but with flowering stems that emerge from the side rather than the centre of the plant. Both *Drosera anglica* and *Drosera intermedia* are less common than the round-leaved sundew. Less common still is a hybrid of *Drosera anglica* and *Drosera rotundifolia*, known as *Drosera × obovate*.

All three British species of sundew, as well as the hybrid, are small, short-lived perennials, not exceeding a few centimetres in height but forming rosettes of sticky, tentacle-covered leaves. All also produce spikes of typically 5-6 small, white of pinkish flowers that are held erect on slender, hairless stems up to 15 centimetres tall. The flowers may be fertilised by pollinators in the normal way, but they can also self-fertilise particularly on dull days when the flowers may not open at all. These plants overwinter as buds of tightly rolled leaves.

Sundews trap and digest small insects and other invertebrates via the 'dew' mucilage exuded by the glandular, reddish hairs ('tentacles') that occur across their leaves. These tentacles respond to the touch and chemical signals of trapped invertebrates, curling inwards to trap and hold prey that adheres to the exudate. Curling of the leaf may take anything from ten seconds to three minutes, the whole leaf lamina often closing slowly around the prey. The tentacles then secrete a range of enzymes that break down the captured prey, absorbing nutrients as a valuable supplement to the limited minerals available from the peaty soils in which they occur.

Other British carnivorous plants include the butterworts (Pinguicula species) living in similar low-nutrient habitats to sundews. Bladderworts (Utricularia species) are also carnivorous plants that live in nutrient-poor freshwater pools where they trap and digest aquatic invertebrates in the bladder-like 'utricles' that give the plants both their common and Latin names.

So, beware when you next venture into the bog... there may be an unexpected carnivore lurking underfoot!

SEPTEMBER

MELLOW FRUITFULNESS

IT IS THAT time of year when nature's fruits are ripening all around us. In ages gone by, this would have been a time of harvesting the literal fruits of the landscape, hedgerows and forests, supplementing crops grown on fertile soils.

In the hedgerows, tresses of blackberries now ripe for the picking tumble on thorny stems. Scratches and stained fingers are small prices to pay for the rich flavour and hue of a piping hot blackberry and apple crumble; just thinking about it is making me hungry! In former times, the blackberries would also be preserved for the long, literally fruitless months ahead. This was not in modern-day freezers, but in preserving jars after boiling to create

near-sterile conditions or as a tasty jam. In years gone by, I have also
preserved them in the form of bramble rum: a delicious concoction involving
blackberries, dark rum and demerara sugar as a variant on the better-known
sloe gin. Perhaps not quite a traditional means of sustenance during those
barren months, but certainly one to warm the heart and, with that rich purple
hue, all of the senses.

And sloes too! Though reaching their best after the fall's first frosts,
when the fruit's purple sheen takes on a patina-like blush, the blackthorn
hedges are already heavy by September with the promise of a fine crop.

In some hedgerows, the closely related bullace – a variety of plum – can
also be found, spherically shaped and larger than the sloe. Though still acidic
in flavour, the sweetness of the bullace comes through like the sloe with full
ripening as the autumn progresses.

Cherries too are to be found, if you can find them ripening before the
birds tune into them. Many mammals too make use of wild cherries as an
important food source. Also, of course, the delicate pink flowers of wild cherry
trees decorate hedgerows and copses in springtime, the ephemeral vista of the
cherry blossom particularly prized in Japanese culture.

Other fruitful riches are to be found in the form of crab apples, cascading
from trees that have also yielded pretty white-pink flowers earlier in the
season.

Tumbling in the lower levels of hedges and scrub are rosehips, brilliant
red and with so many uses. I well recall collecting them in the early 1960s for
the production of rose hip syrup, then still widely produced in homes and used
as a vitamin-rich supplement: for vitamin C in particular to ward off winter
colds. Rosehips can also be used for many other purposes, including as herbal
teas or cold beverages, as wine, as a jam or marmalade, as a jelly or soup, in
pies, or as an addition to bread. Rosehips can also be used to make pálinka,
the traditional Hungarian fruit brandy popular in Hungary, Romania, and
some other countries. Rosehips can also be eaten directly, though require
careful preparation that importantly includes removing the hairy and irritant
seeds inside the red fruity layer. Rather naughtily, I do also remember
collecting the hairy seeds hidden within the fruit to put down people's necks as
itching powder in those long-gone days!

The hazel bushes too bear their crop of nuts, drying from green to dark and
woody brown, each a perfect container preserving the nut within to be enjoyed
throughout the long winter months ahead by people and squirrels alike.

Not to mention crops of sweet chestnuts, the dark nuts revealed by breaking open the green, spiky outer sheathes as they fall from mature trees. They too have their own protective and preservative woody sheathes providing nutrition, flavour and wonderful aroma when roasted in the months to come.

Some elderberries are still hanging on, though many have dropped, those doing so over water gladly intercepted by hungry fish. Beech nuts, haws, guelder and so many more are fruitful in this mellow season of declining day length.

The riverbanks, hedgerows and copses hold many more riches besides, many no longer regarded as worth collecting if indeed their diverse culinary and medicinal uses are remembered at all. After all, when you can order groceries and pharmaceuticals online for delivery to the door, why would you?

But I do wonder and worry about what a store of natural wisdoms we are losing, and with it our respect and value for the natural world that bore us and which we depend upon for our future security and life opportunities.

CANNIBAL GHOSTS

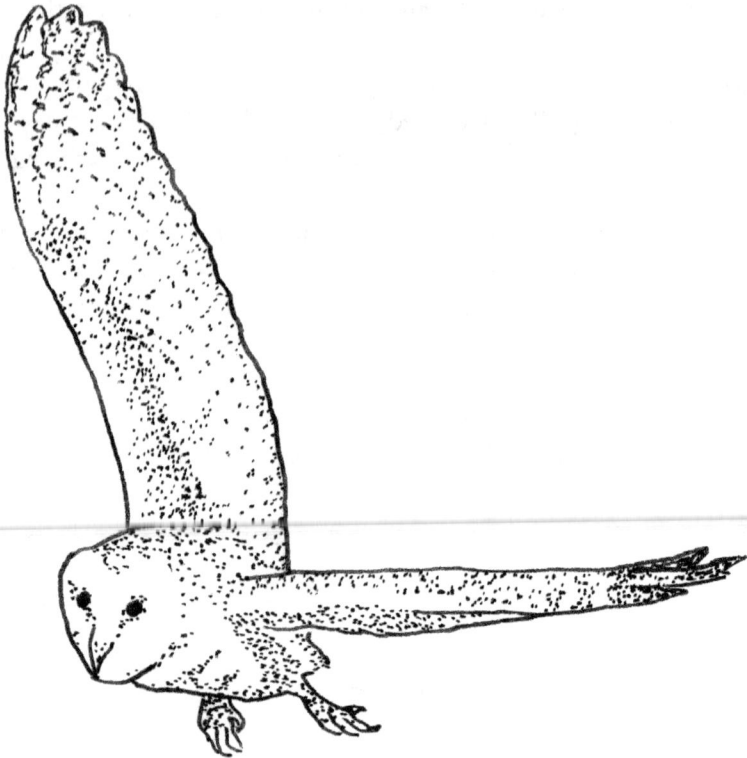

ONE OF THE many beautiful sights greeting those who sit out by rivers into dusk, or during milder earlier afternoons on shorter winter days, is the vison of a white ghost silently quartering riparian meadows and drainage channels.

Ethereally pale and spectrally silent, the barn owl glides on broad wings, face-downwards scanning with discerning ears and eyes for signs betraying small rodents – mice, voles, shrews and some larger mammals – as well as small birds secreted in the turf below. Sometimes, the barn owl will plunge down, talons first. The hunt is not always successful, and so the bird takes to the air once again to renew its surveillance.

The barn owl (*Tyto alba*) is widespread in Britain. In fact, it is the most widespread terrestrial bird species in the world, occurring in every continent with the exception of Antarctica. Barn owls are medium-to-large birds with a wingspan of 80-95 centimetres (31-37 inches), their upper surfaces covered in browny-cream or buff feathers and with a white underside. These owls are predators, hunting farmland and grassland as well as marine and intertidal wetlands for suitable live prey animals. The bird is distinctive and charismatic, both eyes forward-facing and set in a heart-shaped face that focuses sound to its highly sensitive ears. Barn owls are also largely sedentary, not migrating but remaining loyal to a preferred territory. Fledgling barn owls generally disperse only relatively short distances, relocating a few kilometres at most from where they fledged particularly along river corridors.

Like many birds, and particularly predatory bird species (raptors), barn owls suffered declines throughout the twentieth century due to a combination of habitat changes but also the bioaccumulation of organochlorine pesticides such as DDT that were widely used in the 1950s and 1960s. However, with better controls on usage of these and other pesticides, barn owl numbers in Britain appear to have increased since the mid-1990s.

The breeding strategy of the barn owl may appear strange but is a flexible adaptation to cope with varying prey availability. Barn owls begin to breed when they are around one-year old. Male barn owls perform elaborate displays, part of which entails the male bird hovering and dangling his feet in front of the female. From that point onwards, around three-quarters of mating pairs remain together for life. The mating pair builds a nest in a suitably protected niche. This may be a hole in a tree, in undisturbed buildings such as barns and outbuildings or ruins (hence the common name of the species), and sometimes in mines, cliffs or quarries. The owl pair lay and brood between 4 and 7 eggs, laid at intervals over several days. The eggs are incubated for 30-31 days.

Juvenile barn owls hatch at intervals of two or three days, with hatching for the first and last owlets being as much as two or even three weeks apart. This means that the youngsters will be at different growth stages, and with a cascade of sizes. Both adult barn owls hunt for food, initially torn into strips for their chicks. At two weeks old, the growing nestlings can swallow small rodents whole.

The larger, older and stronger owlets are at an advantage competing for food brought to the nest by parent birds. The smaller and weaker youngest chicks tend to die when prey is limited. Perhaps more amazingly, the larger owlets will turn cannibal with food in short supply feasting on their younger siblings!

Cruel though this cannibalistic tendency may appear, it is an adaptation to maximise the survival of the species during years of feast or famine. In a favourable year, many more young owls will fledge after 50-55 days to bolster populations. By contrast, when food resources are sparse, the strongest survive at the expense of the runts. In most years, only around half of the chicks survive to fledge.

Starvation is believed to be the principal cause of mortality of owls after fledging, particularly amongst young and inexperienced birds as they disperse. It is also a principal cause of mortality amongst older birds, both during severe winter weather as well as in the late winter through to early spring period when small mammal numbers and winter temperatures are at their lowest.

The oldest recorded age of a barn owl in Europe is over 21 years: a wise old cannibal ghost indeed!

STRENGTH IN NUMBERS

THE COMMON REED (*Phragmites australis*) is known by many local
names. One of these is 'Norfolk reed', though this is one of the most
widely globally distributed of all flowering plants occurring in fresh and
brackish wetlands from the tropics to temperate zones in both the north and
south hemispheres.

These familiar reeds are tall plants with hollow stems that are green
when young but that age into a golden hue as they dry. Atop the stems from
August to October appear large, feathery flower spikes, initially dark purple
in colour but fading to brown with age. The flowers form seeds. However,
the spread and reproduction of the common reed usually entails it expanding
across damp ground through creeping rhizomes (underground stems). These
reeds form stands that may be very extensive indeed, often dominated by this
single species.

Looking at a single reed stem, which can be as much as 6 metres (nearly

20 feet) tall but more normally up to a more modest 3 metres (nearly 10 feet), one is impressed by its delicacy and apparent fragility with a diameter averaging only 0.5 to 1.5 centimetres (0.2 to 0.6 inches). One could imagine a puff of wind snapping it off in a heartbeat; in fact, individual reed stems are easy to snap in the fingers if bent on a short radius.

However, reeds have superpowers. The first is their flexibility, even the strongest wind seeing them bend, twist and turn to dissipate potentially destructive forces. Their second and greater superpower is that they are colony-forming species, some reedbeds spanning as much as a kilometre square. These extensive reedbeds act like huge buffers dissipating the energy of even massive storms. Not only do the reedbeds survive, but they perform important services in buffering adjacent water bodies, landscapes, livestock and wildlife from extreme weather.

Within a reedbed in a gale, one can find a zone of tranquillity whilst the reed stems gyrate wildly above and around you. The tight, dome-shaped nests of willow warblers woven close to the ground are cossetted within the sanctuary of reed stands, their tiny eggs – three eggs weigh about the same as a penny – brooded unperturbed by surrounding atmospheric chaos. The eggs are brooded and the chicks are fed by both parent birds.

Beds of common reed provide important habitat for many more bird species, including some that are rare or threatened, such as the bittern, marsh harrier and bearded tit. Reedbeds also host a diversity of invertebrate life, including many rare or endangered species of moth, beetle, bug, fly, spider, wasp and bee. These form a larder for predatory species occurring not only within and around reedbeds but across wider landscapes and waterscapes. This invertebrate wealth also represents a reservoir of pollinators and predators of pest organisms

It is this strength in numbers of 'water reeds' that has been exploited as a thatching material for centuries, most significantly across Europe. Thatching today uses this species of reed harvested from many places, including commercial reedbeds cut on a rotational basis in Norfolk but also harvested from places such as Austria, China, France, Hungary, Poland, Romania, Turkey and Ukraine. Skilled thatchers select reeds of a length, strength and other properties appropriate to the specific location and need. Straight reeds make for the best thatching materials, and younger plants too as older material becomes dry and brittle. Reed-thatched roofs typically last between 25 and 40 years, though can last longer.

Stands of common reed are also important for many other reasons, including dissipating the potentially destructive energy of spate flows, trapping sediment and forming soil. They can serve as fodder for livestock. They also sequester carbon from the atmosphere, influence the local microclimate, and play host to water purification processes, as well as attenuating some air pollutants. Reeds also have artistic uses, visually and as a resource for weaving and other crafts. Beds of common reeds are also components of distinctive and aesthetic landscapes.

The strength and value of the common reed stems not so much from individual plants but as a result of the collective mass and functions of the reedbed, in natural, woven or thatched forms. Many in the natural and human worlds benefit greatly from this strength in numbers.

THE EDIBLE RIVER

W E LIVE IN strange times, certainly when compared with much of
our history. Today, food and herbs are easily accessible and largely
affordable from supermarkets and other shops. They are even potentially
ordered online in the middle of the night. But, of course, supermarkets and
online suppliers were not always there. For most of our history, as hunter-
gatherers and in settled societies alike, we have lived off the land. The river
was a major store of edible goodies.

Fish, varying in texture and flavour, fed us. So too did wildfowl in their
season, including their eggs as well as meat. We used the down of some species
too. Many other animals too would fill an empty stomach or clothe a cool
skin.

But it is amongst the riverine plants and fungi that most people would
derive food and flavourings to meet their daily needs.

In the river itself, watercress was and remains a popular salad plant. On
wet meadows, the springtime cuckoo flower (or lady's smock or milkmaids)
is another cress-like plant that is entirely edible and can be served in salads or
blanched as a vegetable. So too are hairy bittercress, common scurvygrass,
wintercress, shepherd's purse and a range of other crucifer plants. Every part
of the dandelion too is edible, from the root to the leaves and the flowers.

In their season, riverside elder bushes yield their purple-black berries and, before that, their white florets; both are still collected to this day for culinary purposes. Blackberries too, of course, and the rosehips of the dog rose glowing red in the autumn, not to mention sloes on autumnal blackthorn bushes.

For flavourings, not to mention some medicinal purposes, the river yields up a smorgasbord of water mint, tansy, wild hops, horseradish and wormwood, and the pungent-smelling ramsons (or wild garlic) is a springtime treat.

Many is the stinging nettle I have eaten, picked young and cooked much like spinach to yield a tasty, dark green vegetable dish that is also a source of many minerals and vitamins. But various species of mallow can also be treated the same way too.

Other waterside plants may be quite obvious sources of food, such as the wild cherry and crab apple. But the young April leaves of hawthorn too have a nutty taste and may be added to salads, and their autumnal red berries, or hawes, yield a jelly when simmered. Various chenopod plants, such as fat hen and good king Henry, can also be eaten as leaf or, rather like asparagus, as early shoots. So too chickweed, which can be eaten whole as the leaves are rather too small to separate and the stems are soft. And the early shoots of the tall rose bay willowherb and also hogweed (also known as cow parsnip) are other plants that can be cooked and eaten á al asparagus.

Ground ivy is one of many plants that can be stewed as a tea. Even various thistle species can be stewed up as vegetables.

This is of course just skimming the surface of available riverside food, and before even turning our attention to the myriad fungi to be found there.

Some notes of caution are necessary. There are some toxic species that the lay collector may mistake for their desired species. You also require the landowner's permission to forage too. And, of course, you must treat scarcer species with respect and leave them well alone.

However, the point is that food and flavours abound. We have lost much of our traditional wisdom about the everyday culinary, not to mention medicinal, folklore and other wisdoms of our forebears, cosseted as we are by modern-day conveniences. Not that I hanker after scouring the riverbank 24/7 just to feed the family!

But I wonder to what extent our modern lifestyles and expectations have inadvertently blinded us to nature's abundance and, frankly, how long we'd survive if left to forage for ourselves?

THE JOY OF FISH TWITCHING

I HAVE, FOR the thick end of seven decades, been in thrall as a scientist, angler, pet fish keeper and 'fish twitcher' to fish and other aquatic life lurking beneath the surface film.

What is 'fish twitching'? Is it contagious?

It is not generally thought unduly weird for people to get excited about looking for terrestrial organisms: birds and mammals, flowers and butterflies, or reptiles and fungi. In the birding world, 'twitching' is widely accepted, if occasionally considered eccentric, with British bird 'twitchers' far from a scarce breed as evidenced by the million-plus membership of the Royal Society for the Protection of Birds (RSPB). Birding is also of substantial economic value through investments in equipment, travel, accommodation, publications and time. Good healthy physical and mental exercise it is too, also serving to provide valuable evidence of environmental health.

I consequently find it odd that, when the water's surface film lies between observer and observed, the small but growing 'fish twitching' community is thought even odder than their birding, fungi foraying, botanising and generally drier counterparts!

This is further evidence of a false division in perception of the importance of fishes relative to other wildlife. Whilst Britain's freshwater fishes are of acknowledged importance for sport and food, and their distribution has been significantly rearranged for those purposes, our fishy wealth nevertheless constitutes an inherently and functionally important part of our national fauna. Why are there no fishy equivalents of the RSPB, Plantlife, Buglife, the Earthworm Society of Britain and other such dedicated groups of enthusiasts?

There is, though, a relatively recent growth in interest in 'fish twitching'. I have played some small role in encouraging this through my books, magazine articles and television work, as the underwater world is a rich and freely accessible resource for the curious amateur or obsessed specialist alike.

All the patient observer needs is a suitable vantage point over still or flowing waters, and the patience and persistence to focus through the surface film. A good pair of polarising sunglasses to cut through surface glare helps greatly. It is also important to remain still, or to walk with soft footfalls, avoiding sharp movements or bright clothes advertising your presence as a potential predator. Keeping the cover of tall vegetation behind you removes your silhouette from the horizon, helping approach fish before they detect you.

Focus through the water on areas of the riverbed or aquatic vegetation. With some luck and diligence, you may begin to pick out the gentle swaying of a trout holding station in flowing water, the dark shapes of a barbel or chub ghosting across the gravel between the cover of stands of vegetation, or other wondrous creatures. During warm days of summer, the dark forms of chub are often seen cruising in surface layers of rivers, often enticed to intercept offerings of bread scraps. In still and slowly flowing waters, crimson-finned rudd may be observed doing the same. The dark and elongated form of a pike, still as death with barely a quiver of fins, may perhaps be glanced as it waits in ambush for smaller fishy prey.

Other tell-tale signs of fish activity in still waters are explosions of bubbles as tench, bream or other fish sift through soft sediment for food items down in the dark depths, most commonly at dawn or dusk. In these crepuscular hours, you may also see fish such as roach and bream 'priming', as they swim to the surface to take a gulp of air to adjust their buoyancy when starting to feed. Or maybe you will spot a surface 'explosion' as a shoal of small fry scatters in frenzy as a posse of hungry perch strikes at them from beneath.

No special access, equipment or investment is required for the enjoyment of the nascent 'fish twitcher', who is rewarded for a little patience by sight of the goings on of formerly unsuspected and underappreciated fishy fauna. Chances are substantially elevated by going out with a more experienced 'twitcher'.

In some places, 'fish twitching' has greater importance. Think of the number of pubs or sites in the British Isles named 'salmon leap' or similar. In India, many temples have sacred pools containing fish of spiritual significance but also tourism value. Trout finning the Derbyshire Wye running through the town of Bakewell or the River Test at Stockbridge are part of the day's experience for visitors.

With care and patience, keeping safe, and ideally also some guidance from more experienced 'twitchers', this is all healthy fun and a great way to appreciate the everyday wonder of nature locally and in the raw.

OCTOBER

AUTUMN COLOURS

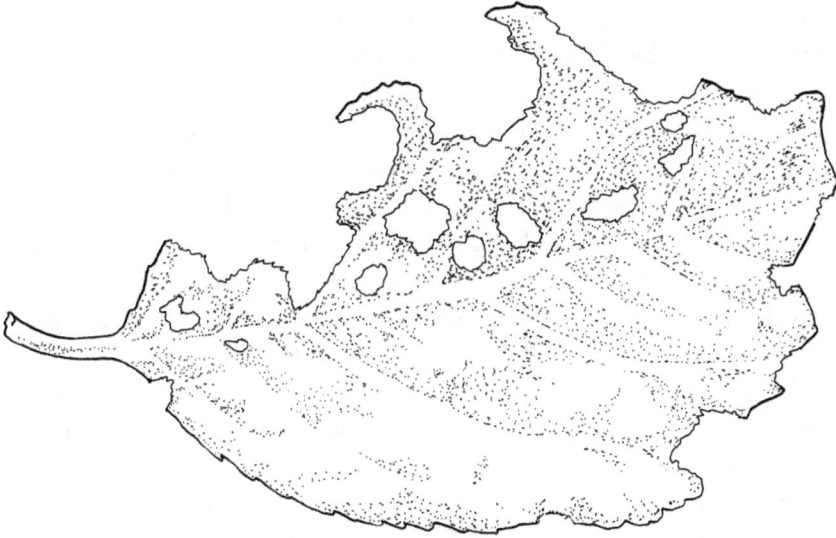

AFTER A SUMMER rich in green hues displayed by lush vegetation, the contracting nights, cooler days and chillier frosty nights mark a change and, with it, leaves fade into flamboyant, burnished tones with the turning of the seasons. Russet, scarlet, yellow and other pastel hues are a joy to the eye that is embedded in cultural celebrations around the temperate world.

There is beauty in all of nature, most visible in autumnal colours, though the reason for this change may be more mundane. The greenery of summer is due to the presence of the pigment chlorophyll in leaf cells, capturing energy from the sun that is used to split water, fusing liberated hydrogen ions with carbon dioxide captured from the air to produce sugars and release oxygen gas as a waste. Sugars constitute the primary organic molecules from which all other organic substances fundamental to life are subsequently synthesised. The alchemy of photosynthesis, harnessing energy in the form of light emitted by the sun, is what powers not only trees and other green plants but, ultimately, virtually all life on Earth, connected as we all are through complex food webs.

But, come the autumn, lowering light intensity makes photosynthetic production less effective and renders soft tissues more vulnerable to degradation by frost and other factors. The environmental signals of day length and night temperature combine to change the metabolism of plants. Trees, perennial herbs and grasses native to temperature regions have evolved to shut down photosynthetic processes in dispensable organs – leaves – resorbing the valuable chemicals that they contain. There is no longer an investment in production of fresh chlorophyll. This leads to the progressive breakdown and reduction in concentration of this green pigment, revealing the colours of the many other chemicals present within the leaves. Each plant species has its own unique colour spectrum according to the proportions of more stable yellow xanthophylls and flavonols, orange carotenoids, and red or purple anthocyanins contained in its leaves. Trees also pump waste products, known as tannins, into the leaf at this time of transition, adding to the brown colour before leaf drop. This serves as a kind of 'detox' for the host plant.

Having resorbed as many useful substances as possible, deciduous trees release hormones triggering production of a compound known as abscisic acid that stimulates development of a seal of corky cells at the leaf bases, the so-called abscission zone, prompting them to fall off. This process traps residual chemicals in the leaves before they fall, also stemming water loss.

Though discarded ostensibly as waste as plants shut down for the winter, or die back entirely if annual, fallen leaves release nutrient substances back into the soil as they are broken down by countless small animals and microorganisms. Rather than a waste, the constituents of the fallen leaves and withered vegetations acts as a fertiliser for the coming year.

In many locations across Britain, the autumn colours of leaves are a significant tourist attraction. This includes, for example, open days at Westonbirt Arboretum in Gloucestershire. The Forest of Dean, also in Gloucestershire, also draws people as does the Ashdown Forest in Sussex, Stourhead on the Wiltshire/Somerset border, amongst many more localities both formal and informal. As a child, kicking through golden-brown carpets of fallen leaves in sweet chestnut woodland was a seasonal joy. In fact, the term 'leaf peeping' was coined from 1966 in the United States, where it is also known as 'fall color tourism', to describe the activity of people travelling to observe, photograph or otherwise enjoy autumnal colours as the leaves of trees change colour. Similar quiet enjoyment of the dramatic vista of changing leaf colour in forests is also prevalent in other nations known, for example, as *ruskaretki* in Finland, *momijigari* (hunting autumn/red leaves) in Japan, *dan pung ku gyeong* in South Korea, and *shangye* in China.

Various spiritual meanings are attributed to leaves, assigned by shape and colour. Some relate to the changing hues of autumn. Many such seasonal traditions relate to turning and falling leaves signifying the cycle of life. Falling leaves are said by dream interpreters to symbolise letting go. Some belief systems see the falling of leaves are a reminder of the evanescence of life.

Whatever meanings are imputed to leaves, and their changing colours and surrender to gravity when their seasonal productive work is done, nature is nothing if not economical and efficient and so there are important ecological functions at play beneath this veneer of beauty. But that is no reason not to stand, stare and admire, taking in yet another of the temperate world's many inspiring and characteristic vistas.

FROZEN WINGS

THE FIRST MAJOR frosts of the year, most often in the latter half of
October in southern England, mark a sharp transition between autumn
and winter.

Aside from the dramatic morphing from greens into burning colours and
subsequent fall of leaves from deciduous trees, flighted insect life is also stilled
as the cold air is robbed of the gaudy wings of butterflies.

The adult forms of many, but far from all, late summer and early autumn
butterflies simply die with the encroaching cold. However, different species of
butterfly deploy a diversity of overwintering strategies for survival throughout
the colder months.

Some butterfly species overwinter as eggs, including some of the
hairstreaks, skippers and blues. Many more overwinter as caterpillars that
find refuge from frost and become dormant, including a variety from the
skipper, blue, fritillary and brown families. Many members of the white
butterfly family overwinter in chrysalis form, including the large white,
small white, green-veined white, orange tip and wood white, as do some
butterflies from other families. However, some more robust British butterflies
– brimstones, small tortoiseshell, peacock and comma – overwinter in adult
form.

And then there are some butterflies that simply die in the cooling British climate – the painted lady, red admiral and clouded yellow amongst them – relying on repopulation of these isles in the coming year by migration from continental Europe, though a few may overwinter as adults particularly with the warming global climate, and some may make or attempt a reverse, southward migration.

Of these overwintering adult butterflies, the habits of the comma (*Polygonia c-album*) are perhaps the most remarkable. Adult small tortoiseshell and peacock butterflies seek dry shelter away from frost in places such as wood piles and crevices in rocks and trees or outhouses. Whilst the comma too will hibernate in these sheltered spots, it can also be found hibernating in more open vegetation, even at time with frosted wings. With its scalloped wing edges and the cryptic mottled brown colour of its underwings, adult comma butterflies hang amongst dead leaves, particularly of their major food plants that include nettles, brambles, hops, elm, willow or currant.

Comma butterflies were once a localised and generally rare sight in Britain. In the mid-1800s, the butterfly was confined to the Welsh Marches. The decline of the species was believed to be linked to reductions in the farming of hops, the then-preferred food plant of comma caterpillars. However, commas from that low point adapted their larval diet to a preference for nettles, as well as the range of other plant species noted above. Since then, the butterfly's range has progressively expanded such that comma butterflies are now found throughout England and Wales and into Scotland, particularly in suitable woodland clearings, along hedgerows and in gardens. Unlike the widespread population declines observed for many British butterfly species, the comma represents a butterfly success story having substantially increased in range and population size over the past 40 years. The butterfly's northward expansion may have been aided by the warming British climate.

Adult comma butterflies have been recorded in every month of the year in Britain, even in mid-winter as, although hibernating butterflies normally will not take to the wing between November and late February, the warmth of sunny days even in the depths of winter may be sufficient to wake them from dormancy. Adult commas surviving the winter are amongst the earliest butterflies to take flight in Britain.

Waking adult commas might remain on the wing between March and the end of May, laying their eggs on food plants. Voracious caterpillars hatch from these eggs, growing on before pupating and resulting in an emergence of fresh flying adult commas typically between June and July. It is not uncommon, particularly in warmer and extended summers, for some of the earliest emerging butterflies from this new generation to then produce a second generation that emerges as flying adults from late-August or into September. Surviving adults then overwinter to repeat the cycle.

Whilst the upper sides of the wings of the comma are a deep orangey-brown colour with black markings, the underside is mottled in browns helping the butterfly merge with dead leaves when the wings are closed. At the centre of the underside of the hindwing, comma butterflies have a tiny white mark resembling a comma punctuation mark, from which this fascinating butterfly derives its common name.

PARADISE LOST?

COMPRESSED BY THE telescope of history, summers were always sunny way back when, just as winters were always crisp with snow. Wildlife was also profuse, but that comparison with today is far from an illusion.

Denied access to fishing and other freedoms in early 2020 due to the ravages of the pandemic, much of my enjoyment of the local watery environment beyond daily walks has been vicarious. My 'sport' has largely comprised mining memories of times long gone.

In the early 1960s, I lived in Kent, later spending the early 1970s in Sussex before disappearing into the big city when going up to university. Roaming the countryside, I grew acquainted with small water bodies abounding on the clay. Some were dew ponds, others were marl pits and some were bomb craters, all a legacy of former times. All seemed to host families of water voles – 'Ratty' from *The Wind in the Willows* – frequently seen paddling the calm surface at dusk. Moorhens were ubiquitous, newts crept in thick water weed, and small fishes abounded in at least some secret watery wonderlands.

I suspect virtually all these minute wildlife oases are now lost. Most will have silted up or been filled in long ago, serving no use in modern farming landscapes. A minority might have been enlarged and stocked with bigger fish to meet bigger expectations.

But memories of the wealth of three-spined sticklebacks, male fish brighter than peacocks in their spawning regalia, swim on with great affection in my mind. So too those pools hosting glorious little bronze-flanked crucians, or the occasional rudd or tench. Many or most if not all these bijou water bodies were brightened by the dance of damselflies and the alarm cries of moorhens hiding in marginal weed stands or under tumbling willows. There were so many other inspiring and enduring vignettes.

I have a hankering for things simpler, slower and smaller in scale in every regard, as do many of my increasingly crusty colleagues. I wish I could find such a neglected pool again today, hunting mini-monsters whilst being eaten alive by mosquitoes. However, today's profoundly changed landscape economics hold no value for these seemingly inconsequential watering holes, razed under a model of progress rewarding only intensive farming, housing, roads and other hard infrastructure.

These oases now live on almost exclusively as ghosts in my imagination. Yet, whilst many idylls romanticise past times that never really existed, those 1960s pondscapes were as real as the air I breathe today.

It was no illusion that wildlife was formerly more profuse. For all the massed nature we see on television, did you know that 96% of the global biomass of mammals now comprises humans and our livestock? Scientific studies also find that, since just 1970, populations of many wild animal species have more than halved. The average rate of loss of vertebrate species over the last century is 100 times higher than background rates, insect populations are experiencing precipitous decline, and biodiversity loss is proceeding at such a rate that we are facing a mass extinction event. Authoritative global surveys found that 75% of the global land surface is already significantly altered, and over 85% of global wetland area has been lost. The loss of those small but important watery oases of wildlife, once so ubiquitously scattered across the southern English landscape in the distant days of my childhood, is of far more than nostalgic value.

If the pause imposed on global human activity in 2020 has any meaningfully positive legacy, it should be that it causes us to reflect and chose a different pathway of development that values nature not merely for its inherent values, but as the principal and vital underpinning resource supporting future human security and opportunity. That unique moment in human history can give us pause to choose, indeed demand, a different pathway into a future of greater stability and prospects supported by recovering natural systems. We have to seize this unprecedented opportunity to rebuild our much-degraded natural world not just for its beauty and inherent worth but as the irreplaceable life support system upon which all of our futures depend.

The mantra of that time was "*Building back better*", and we should seize upon that in terms of the real biophysical foundations of the edifice of a more fulfilling future, not merely a swift return to short-term and ultimately destructive profit-taking based on their systematic liquidation.

With global society now well within the United Nations's 2021-2030 *Decade on Ecosystem Restoration*, there is no excuse for reverting to anachronistic habits perpetuating the serial destruction of natural systems essential for the continuing health, wealth, security and quality of life for all.

Give me, every time, a small pond in a quiet setting over an overstocked lake of near-captive fish set in an otherwise sterile landscape.

ANTS AND SEED
DISPERSAL

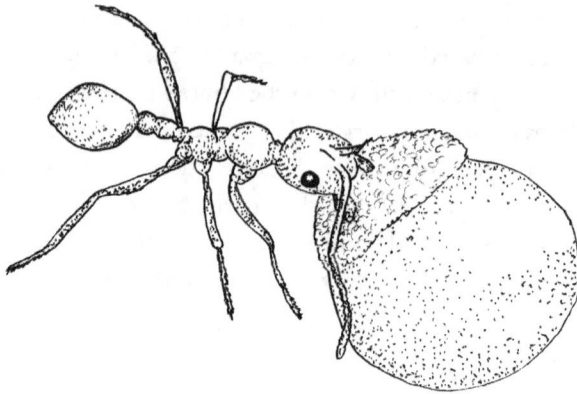

W E HUMANS TEND to overlook the small, apparently less significant life
forms with which we share this complicated world. However, we do
so at our peril, for the work they perform is of not just huge but fundamental
importance.

Take, for example, ants. We know that ants are an important food
source for many species of birds, mammals and other insects as well as reptiles,
amphibians and fish. Also, that they maintain and rebuild soil structure
and porosity, and play important roles in breaking down complex organic
matter, recycling it into bioavailable forms. Lesser known, though nonetheless
fundamentally important, is the role that these small social insects play in the
dispersal and germination of the seeds of plants.

Seed dispersal amongst numerous plant species mediated by ants is in fact
well known and important enough to have its own name: 'Myrmecochory', a
term coined in 1906 by the Swedish naturalist Johan Rutger Sernander (1866-
1944).

For some plants, seed dispersal by ants is not just important but essential.
These are referred to as 'myrmecochorous plants'. A recent study has found that
over 4% of flowering plants are myrmecochorous, so the contribution of ants
to botanical dispersal and wider roles in ecosystem resilience and functioning
is highly significant. Examples of myrmecochorous plants in the UK include
the snowdrop (*Galanthus nivalis*), three-cornered garlic (*Allium triquetrum*),
common cow-wheat (*Melampyrum pratense*), wood anemone (*Anemone*

nemorosa) and various species of violets (*Viola* species).

Many genera and species of ants have been found to be involved in myrmecochory. Myrmecochorous plants commonly rely for dispersal on specific ant species; any old ant will simply not do, though no single myrmecochorous plant has been found to reply only on a single ant species.

The seeds of myrmecochorous plant species tend to have a fleshy outer structure known as an eliosome, which is rich in lipid (fat) as well as protein. This is not only an attractively rich energy source for the foraging ant but, early research is suggesting, may contain chemical signals inducing particular behaviours in ants: in particular necrophoresis (corpse-carrying).

Ants thereby have important roles in transporting seeds, aiding plant dispersal. As ants consume the eliosome, they detach it from the seed and may also scarify the hard seed surface, both processes aiding germination. Sometimes, seeds are dropped after the eliosome is consumed. Other ant species – particularly 'harvester ants' that forage for seeds that are taken back and stored in their nests for consumption particularly by the larvae – may drop some seeds outside of the nest. Whilst some harvester ant species consume the seeds they have gathered, others discard the seeds once the eliosome has been consumed.

As ants are so widespread and abundant across many types of landscape, it is perhaps far from surprising that numerous plants have evolved in concert with them to promote dispersal and germination of their seeds. The benefits of animal-vectored dispersal include averting conflict with other seedlings, reaching new niches in the landscape, and avoiding consumption by other animals. Dispersal by ants can also improve resilience against stresses such as fire, observed particularly for ant species in fire-prone regions of Australia as these insects carry the seeds into nests built below ground. Ants may also drop seeds in microhabitats that are richer in nutrients, further aiding gemination and accelerated growth.

Dispersal of seeds by other groups of animals is well known, particularly those producing fruits and nuts that are consumed by birds, mammal and fish. Other plant seed dispersal mechanisms are found in species producing fruits or seeds that cling to animals (for example cleavers, *Galium aparine*, also known as goosegrass).

But let us not overlook the tiny labourers upon whom fall many of the important yet widely overlooked functions that keep ecosystems healthy, just one aspect of which entails maintaining and extending the range of plants across broad habitat types.

GOSSAMER TIME

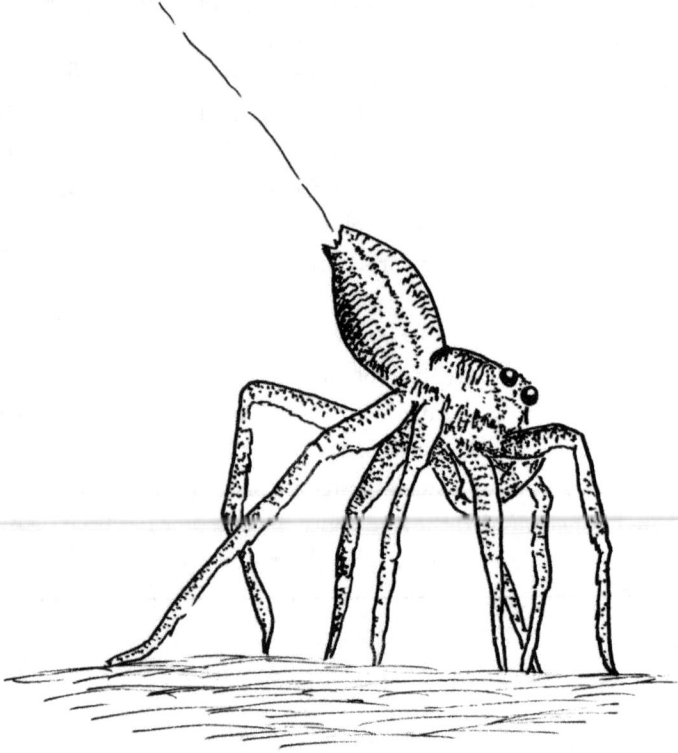

I T WAS ONE of those gloriously bright October days, a high-pressure
weather system painting the sky pale blue with the barest puff of wind.
The sun, warm on the skin after the dawn mists had burned through, belied
the reality of ever-encroaching dusk and the cool fingers of winter reaching out
from the near future.

On the riverbank, grasses and herbs were browned and dried with their
purposes fulfilled for another year. The willows still held their leaves, though
many were now fringed yellow or mottled with brown spots highlighting
their seasonal superfluity.

This last hurrah of receding summer was not mine alone to savour. As
I sat, drowsy in the sunshine, I became aware of gossamer threads around me

billowing skywards from the bankside sward.

This is another of nature's magical times. As leaves start to curl and fall, other creatures are letting out spinnakers to carry them aloft and afar.

Various species of spider undertake this 'ballooning' behaviour, also known as 'kiting', letting out fine silken strands from the vantage points of tall vegetation. When the spiders judge their gossamer threads to be long enough, they release their grip and are borne aloft.

This phenomenon has been known since the time of Greek philosopher and polymath Aristotle (384-322BCE). Charles Darwin, the father of evolutionary theory, expressed his puzzlement on his famous voyage on the Beagle (1831-1836), wondering how these 'aeronaut spiders' reached the ship on their gossamer threads as much as sixty miles off the coast of South America.

Research published since 2013 changed our perception of quite how ingenious this ballooning behaviour really is. Whilst we may only become aware of the Earth's electrical fields when charges build up to such a point that they create lightening, the electrical senses of many species are far more acute. Experiments in which spiders were held in sealed chambers with no air currents found that spiders took off, buoyed on their fine silken strands, when an electric field was switched on. Electrical repulsion on the charged thread provides sufficient lift. When the electric field was turned off, the spiders descended back to earth. Ballooning spiders fly not simply on the wind, much like a boat raising its spinnaker, but on the Earth's electric fields. Spiders have special hair-like sensory organs, known as trichobothria, that detect electric fields in much the same way that human hairs rise in the presence of static electricity. So, when a spider detects a suitably strong electric field, it may climb up a tall twig or blade of grass to let out a silken thread to carry it aloft.

On mass ballooning events, the ground can apparently be covered in mats of silk.

This behaviour has been observed in many species of spider. Although mainly undertaken by spiderlings (young spiders) as a means of dispersal, larger individuals have also been observed doing so. Journeys can vary from a few metres to hundreds of kilometres. Atmospheric samples collected from altitudes of up to five kilometres often include ballooning spiders, and ships in mid-ocean commonly report spider landings. Obviously, mortality is high, though many ballooning species also possess water-repelling legs enabling them to survive afloat on both fresh and salt water, and even to withstand moderate waves. Spiders making safe landfall can have considerable advantages through exploiting new habitats often very far distant from their point of embarkation.

Spiders are not alone in this efficient means of distribution. A number of other small invertebrates too let out fine gossamer threads to be borne aloft by air currents or electric fields. The behaviour is observed amongst spider mites, and also in thirty-one species of lepidoptera (butterflies and moths). Amongst these are some moth species with flightless females, such as the mottled umber (*Erannis defoliaria*) and the winter moth (*Operophtera brumata*), the males of which are seen on the wing in Britain during the winter months of November to February. Female moths divert their energies into egg production rather than flight, attracting male moths by pheromones (hormones released into the air from their flightless bodies) that are carried on night breezes. Flightlessness obviously poses problems for dispersal, overcome by small caterpillars 'ballooning' after crawling to a high point to let out strands of silk carrying the tiny grubs aloft over sometimes prodigious distances.

On a cool and clear October day, under a bright sun and with a light breeze, look out for these tell-tale gossamer strands showing that, whilst some species are hunkering down for the coming winter, others are very much on the move.

NOVEMBER

ALARM CALL

I WAS ROUSED in the near light of early morning by an alarm.
This is not such an unusual experience, you may think. However, this
was no digital bleep nor clockwork clatter pre-set to rouse me from slumber.

This alarm was not only outside, but also had multiple sources.
Something, or somethings, out there was, or were, alarmed!

It took barely seconds to recognise that these were the strident and
urgent "*Chink, chink!*" alarm cries of three, possibly four, blackbirds calling
out a warning echoed by their fellows.

Tumbling out of bed, I looked out the window onto the front drive and
hedges, but the gloom was still too dense to make out much. Falling back
into bed, I hoped for the welcome embrace of sleep but was thwarted by a
subconscious empathy with those continuing alarm cries.

Maybe ten minutes later, I was up and looking out again. In the now-
strengthening half-light, I discerned two male blackbirds between the cars on

our drive, their alarm cries echoed by another blackbird unseen in the hedge and one more secreted in some indeterminate place not so far away.

What I could not see was what had triggered their alarm calls. Our cat was curled up at the foot of the bed, so was not a culprit. Another cat along the street may have been on the prowl, but the birds were pretty familiar with these domestic predators. Probably not the sparrowhawk either as, although it is a regular strafing visitor, the light was still a little muted for this keen-eyed raider. Anyhow, it is generally the excited twittering of smaller birds that signals the presence of this avian predator. More likely a fox, of which we are not in short supply, or some other hunter.

The blackbird's characteristic "*Chink, chink!*" alarm cry, often issued from a high perch, alerts neighbouring birds when danger is spotted, and is generally echoed by adjacent blackbirds as a kind of 'jungle drum' to alert others of the presence of avian, mammalian, human or other potential threats. Often, these alarm vocalisations are accompanied by an agitated flicking of the tail and wings, offering additional visual cues that danger is abroad.

However, another factor may have been at play. By and large, blackbirds are relatively solitary. In their first year, male blackbirds, distinguished by their overall blackness contrasting with the deep brown of female birds, establish a territory that is generally held for the rest of their lives. These territories may be smaller in favourable sites leading to small aggregations of birds, though there is no distinct social structure. Territories are essential for pair formation and nesting, though territorial boundaries loosen when the last broods have fledged and adult birds moult. However, male blackbirds re-establish territories in the late autumn to stake their claim on food resources. They also become highly and aggressively territorial in the spring-to-summer breeding period. The alarm cries are then also part of complex territorial behaviour rather than just the announcement of would-be predators in the neighbourhood.

What may have been occurring in the half-light of that November morning, following a warmer autumn that may have played its part in deferring the early-winter staking of territory, is in fact a bit of a vocal contest between adjacent male blackbirds re-establishing their territories. Often, male blackbirds will also let out their "*Chink, chink!*" alarm cries in the evening, announcing territory ownership and deterring other blackbirds from roosting within the vicinity before night falls. The two blackbirds that I had seen that dim morning were, in fact, both males, and they were on the ground too rather than crying out warnings from a high and exposed vantage point as is generally the case when a predator is sighted.

This seasonal territory-sparring behaviour is compounded by the fact that, although we generally observe blackbirds to be year-round resident birds, at least 12% of the blackbirds present in Britain and Ireland during the winter are immigrants from elsewhere in Europe. Mainly, these birds arrive from Finland, Sweden and Denmark with some also joining from the Netherlands and Germany. Some only pass through, *en route* to wintering grounds in Spain, France and Portugal, but a good number overwinter in Britain.

So, suddenly, as food diminishes with the season, food sources and the territories within which they occur are increasingly contested by swelling numbers of birds. Most likely then, the early morning alarm calls that woke me that late-November were a contested claim or a proclamation of rights by competing male blackbirds for the favourable habitat of our front garden.

SIMPLE PLEASURES

IN A HECTIC world, in which ever-demanding electronic media clamours
for our attention on a host of devices, it is a simple pleasure to take a break.
A walk round the garden; down the lane; better still, wander to the river
bridge and maybe along the riverbank. It is not so much a matter of leaving
all that urgent stimulation behind, but of immersion in a far more sensual and
diverse set of stimuli as the sights, sounds, aromas and textures of the natural
world bathe you in their presence.

It is not without reason that practices such as *shinrin yoku*, the Japanese
practice of 'forest bathing', is attracting attention and increasing numbers of
devotees in the west. Leaving the devices behind to wander quietly in amongst
the trees, sensing the tranquillity, observing nature passively, and allowing its
healing immersion to relax body and mind is soothing, a potent de-stressing
technique co-beneficial for many dimensions of health and wellbeing.

It is not just the trees that do this. For those who love water, ambling
along by the river has at least as much of a pacifying effect. Taking in the hues
and buzz of a meadow, harmonised by the gentle lapping of water, can be just
as much of a balm if you can quieten the mind sufficiently to surrender to the
surroundings.

In a complex world, the simple pleasures really matter.

Pervasive media invading our spaces for much of the rest of life seem intent on marketing dissatisfaction through a playbook of paid advertising that is as familiar as it is relentless. It sells us the message that, if it is only a year old, you should buy the latest model of mobile phone to be seen with as it has more bells and whistles than you will never use or need. It tells us that we should move careers and earn more money to get on in life. It deceives us that you will be a better human being if you upgrade to the latest model of car or computer. Or that, though you may be happy in your normal holiday routine, but there are more exclusive resorts and trips that would be better. Your guests will, apparently, be super-impressed if you buy more expensive food, ingredients and recipe books, though really if you need to impress that kind of guest then perhaps your priorities are a little warped! And the adverts go on and on, suggesting that your well-established musical tastes are 'so yesterday', so you should instead be listening to new artists and purchasing their merchandise. And, as to those clothes and trainers you are wearing... We are bombarded relentlessly with dissatisfaction, with novel market-based solutions destined to become tomorrow's disappointing history when the newest model arrives.

The simple question is one of what fulfils a person. Running on the treadmill of the next new product, feature or thing to be seen with is to be sold a perpetually soon-to-be-outmoded dream. Is new and more always better? Slavishly throwing your income at these chimaeras in the hope of enduring status or satisfaction is to buy into a hollow neoclassical fantasy.

We certainly need a level of material sufficiency – shelter, mobility, and so on – to feel secure. But, beyond a certain *de minimus*, 'things' alone lose their capacity to make us happy. Fascinating research from around the world plots 'happiness', or life satisfaction, against per capita wealth. Whilst methods of calculation differ, the conclusions converge strongly. People in those nations that are the poorest clearly do not enjoy great life satisfaction. Those with sufficient have maximum life satisfaction. But, beyond this zenith, people in nations with increasing per capita income experience declining satisfaction. The focus in these privileged countries shifts away from absolute wealth defined by sufficiency to meet needs, tending towards comparative wealth under which people compare their assets, subconsciously or consciously, with those around them.

This is how that pervasive advertising and subliminal messaging works:

the newest, the latest, the most à la mode, the blingiest, the fastest, the rarest, the prettiest, the loudest... on and on, trapped in an endless treadmill of temporary satisfiers, but hard-wired to longer-term disappointment in a market-driven addiction.

A walk along the river or in a forest is not like that. There is no comparison, nor embedded disappointment. There is no judgement. There is just timeless nature, constant yet ever-changing with seasonal and meteorological factors, uncritical and ever there for quiet observation that unfailingly reveals something new and inspiring.

Simple pleasures, in a far from simple world, are a sanity and sanctuary. Simple pleasures are the source of sufficiency, ever-fulfilling, and an antidote to the market-driven addictions baying constantly for our attention and wealth.

Experience and call it what you will: *Shinrin yoku*, 'green exercise', the joy of walking barefoot over cool grass, the sibilance of water over a weir, the 'biophilia hypothesis', a calming walk or a relaxing fishing session. The evidence of how simple exposure to nature improves cognitive function, brain activity, blood pressure, mental health, physical activity and sleep are as robust as findings about the inverse effects of prolonged disconnection.

For peace of mind, increased physical activity and decreased risk of cardiovascular disease amongst other metrics of physical health and, with it, relief from depression, anxiety and other aspects of mental health, there is no finer nor cheaper cure than losing yourself in the natural world with which we co-evolved.

OUR INVISIBLE FRIEND

I T IS ALL around us, affecting us in so many direct and indirect ways, yet we cannot see it.

Without it, the world as we know it simply could not have come into being, and certainly could not continue as it is.

Sometimes, we welcome it. Other times, we curse it. But mostly, it passes by 'under the radar' of our daily consciousness.

Wind: so diverse that we have a broad lexicon from zephyr to gale, breeze to gust, puff to hurricane, draught to tempest, whisper to jet stream, and many more terms besides. One of my favourite is the very specific Japanese 'matsukaze', meaning the wind ('kaze') in the pines ('matsu').

Wind is the great mixer and transporter of the lower atmosphere, spreading rain and pollen, downy seeds and pollutants, scent and spores, pheromones and dust. Without it, landscapes inland from coasts would be parched deserts, and moist air would not be conveyed into uplands to cool and condense as rain and snow, giving birth to the headwaters of river systems, wetlands and aquifers. Only plants pollinated by insects, birds, bats and spiders could set seed on arid plains, though whether this vegetation could have evolved from wind-pollinated progenitors would have been very doubtful.

Cereal plants from which staple crops derive could not have been fertilised without the aid of air currents to spread pollen.

Even if the animals we exploit today for food, fibre, hides and traction could find alternative vegetation in some mythical 'elsewhere', in the absence of the plains of wind-pollinated grasses with which they evolved and on which we ranch them, our history would have been radically different. Without the trade winds, we would have had no sail-driven era of empire upon which patterns of exploration, resource exploitation, colonisation and technological advancements depended, and from which contemporary globalised trade relationships derive. Nor, if grain substitutes could have been procured, could windmills have been invented to grind flour as a basis for so many staple foods across the world, or to pump water for irrigation or drainage.

History would have been profoundly different were wind not so ubiquitous, carrying warmth from the equator to the poles and moisture around the globe, forming familiar clouds and weather patterns. Had life been able to emerge on a profoundly different planet, it would inevitably have taken a radically divergent evolutionary pathway adapted to quite dissimilar conditions. The emergence of humanity never was a given but would have been vanishingly improbable to the point of impossibility in that very different biogeographical scenario.

But for the gift of wind, washed clothes could not dry, and commonplace cotton and wool fibre from which many of our clothes are made could not have been produced. Fossil fuel reserves generated from compression of plant matter in the carboniferous era would not have been able to form, meaning that our most well-established basic resource for power generation, mobility and polymer production could not have come to be. And, of course, without those long eras of photosynthetic stripping of carbon from the atmosphere, locking it away into immobile forms in the Earth's crust, the carbon-rich atmosphere would have remained too hot for the condensation of oceans and the genesis of life. A windless world would be so very different from the buffered, if increasingly destabilised, climate we enjoy today.

So, when you feel a cooling summer breeze or the icy fingers of a winter's draught, when the lid blows off the recycling bin, tousles your hair or knocks your hat off, or as it knocks over a favourite potted plant or gusts drive rain against the window pane keeping you awake at night, don't forget to give thanks for that invisible friend that makes life possible, rich and rewarding.

Maybe the simplistic wisdom of Mary Poppins – "*Let's go fly a kite!*" – is not such a frivolity. Maybe we all need to feel the tug of the wind on the string of a kite, a sail or fishing line, in our hair or to hear the rattling of milk bottles in their crate, to remind us how remarkable the world in which we live really is, and to give a quiet thanks for the invisible forces that make and maintain it so.

CRONK!

THE PEACE OF a quiet autumn or winter's day may be interrupted by a coarse, guttural *"Cronk!"* from somewhere overhead.

Maybe you have visions of some old crone of a witch flying high on her broomstick. Looking up, you see a large black shape on broad wings paddling across the sky, cronking (also referred to a 'gronking') from time to time. Maybe you think that the witch is a shapeshifter and has transformed to hide her secret.

The common raven (*Corvus corax*) is a large black bird widely distributed across the northern hemisphere. In fact, this species is just one of nine extant raven species across the world, distributed across northern, eastern and southern Africa, the Arabian Peninsula and the Greater Middle East, Australia, United States and Mexico. These various raven species are members of the crow family (Corvidae).

In the British Isles, we have only the one species – the common raven – the largest member of the crow family, up to 68 centimetres (over two feet) long and with a wingspan of up to 150 centimetres (five feet). This large bird is black all over, though showing blue iridescence when viewed closely. It has a large, thick and powerful bill, also black in colour, and its long wings enable it to travel substantial distances showing off a diamond-shaped tail in flight. The common raven is a resident species, not straying far from favoured habitat and remaining there all year. Its habitat preferences are quite broad, spanning woodland, farmland, the coast, uplands as well as urban and suburban areas.

Ravens eat animal matter. They favour carrion, but will also take small live or dead mammals, birds and their eggs, as well as insects and other invertebrates.

But, like those high-flying witches, all manner of myths surround the raven. Aside from its coarse "Cronk!", its large, dark form and appetite for dead animal matter, ravens are highly intelligent and playful. Sadly, this had led some to believe that the presence of ravens is an ill omen. Indeed, a long-established collective noun for raven is an 'unkindness', alternative collective names including a 'treachery, and a 'conspiracy'.

The Welsh and Irish word for the raven is 'Bran'. In Welsh mythology, the god Bran the Blessed is a guardian of Britain, for whom the raven is a totem. Bran ordered for his own head to be cut off, after which it could still speak words of prophecy. Legend has it that Bran's head was buried beneath Tower Hill at the Tower of London. The presence of ravens at the Tower is an echo of this legend. A prophecy says that if the ravens ever leave the tower, Britain will fall (so their wings are clipped, just in case!)

A Cornish myth is that King Arthur, the legendary guardian of Britain, did not really die but was magically transformed into a raven.

Old myths have it that the Irish goddess Morrighan had a number of different guises, including taking the form of a raven in her aspect as goddess of war. Scottish legend tells of a hag called Cailleach took the form of a number of birds, including the raven, and feasted on men's bodies. Odin, the chief of the Norse gods, was accompanied by a pair of ravens – Hugin (thought) and Munin (memory) – that would fly far and wide to bring news to Odin; one of Odin's names, Hrafnagud, means the 'Raven God'. Likewise, ravens feature in the Old Testament: the raven was the first bird Noah is said to have sent to look for land.

There are many more myths and legends attributing various benign and malign aspects to the raven, with a wealth of raven folklore found right here in the British Isles. However, beyond the fables and allegories, this is a fascinating bird that, despite its large size, strong beak, hoarse "Cronk!" and appetite for carrion, is a playful and intelligent creature fully deserving of our respect.

OUT FOR SIGHT; OUT OF MIND?

W E ARE AT that time of year when we can expect deluges of late-autumn or winter rains to swell the river, perhaps to inundate remaining floodplains (and buildings and infrastructure incautiously constructed upon them) and to turn paths into quagmires. And, as the seasonal torrents continue to fall, often is heard the cry " *When will it ever stop raining?*"

As anglers, walkers, gardeners or just people wandering to the shop to pick up the morning newspaper, we may feel that we have had quite enough of this seemingly interminable precipitation. In fact, looking out over the sodden river valley, it may look like that too. But it is what is going on unseen way beneath our feet that really matters.

The term 'aquifer' describes underground layers of water-bearing strata in the upper Earth's crust. These strata can comprise permeable rock (such as chalk of the North and South Downs), fractured rock (such as the Jurassic limestone of the Cotswolds) or unconsolidated materials (gravel, sand or silt). Where groundwater in these aquifers is closer to the surface, we may extract it from wells or from pools in depressions in the landscape, which may vary in level with the seasons as the 'water table' rises or recedes. The nature of the stratum in which groundwater occurs also affects the chemistry of the water, with harder water withdrawn from chalk and limestone and softer water from sand, gravel and silt.

The science of this underground water – hydrogeology – is complex. But one of the realities is that, like water in a bath, pond or cistern, groundwater resources are finite and depend on recharge. Across the world, there is widespread over-drafting (extraction of groundwater beyond recharge rates), creating all sorts of problems.

A more tangible problem is that over-extraction of groundwater can result in a shortage of water available for public supply, hence drought-related hosepipe bans and other restrictions. A deeper problem is that groundwater is also the source of a great deal of the flow in rivers, and so over-extraction from and depression of aquifer levels can stem life-giving flows in our streams and river systems with major consequences for wildlife and downstream human uses.

At the coast, excessive groundwater withdrawal can result in salty water intruding: there are regions of India in which I have worked where villages and farmland have had to be abandoned as much as ten kilometres inland as the groundwater has become too salty due to subterranean saltwater ingress consequent from excessive pumping and depletion of formerly fresh subterranean water reserves. Also, when working in China, I learned that the super-fast bullet train in the North China Plain can't now run at high speed as over-extraction from the underlying aquifer had resulted in land subsidence, meaning that the rails are no longer sufficiently straight.

We abuse this unseen wealth with some jeopardy.

Dependence on groundwater varies geographically with the permeability of underlying rock. Across England as a whole, groundwater is the source for approximately one-third of water extracted for public supply. It is also drawn upon locally, albeit to a lesser overall extent, in the generally harder and less permeable geologies of Wales and Scotland. Chalk and sandstones are the most productive from this point of view, with fractured limestone also a significant source for public supply. More widely, multiple private supplies bore down to and pump from this rich underground resource to serve agricultural, domestic and industrial uses.

We may look out of the window at yet more rain falling, seeing the surging river or the saturated floodplain, and be tempted to ask " *Haven't we had enough?*" But spare a thought for the fact that it is what permeates slowly into underlying aquifers, through soil we have often compacted into impermeability or paved over impeding the steady percolation of water, that is critical for recharging a resource that is unseen, its value often unappreciated, but that we rely upon to see us safely through the year ahead when balmy, drier weather returns.

DECEMBER

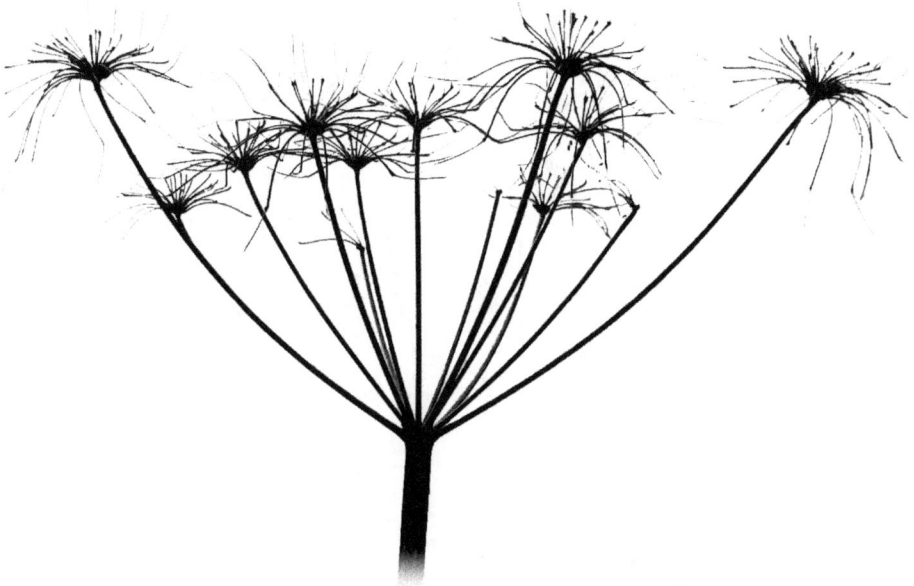

THE SPIKY
SHAPESHIFTER

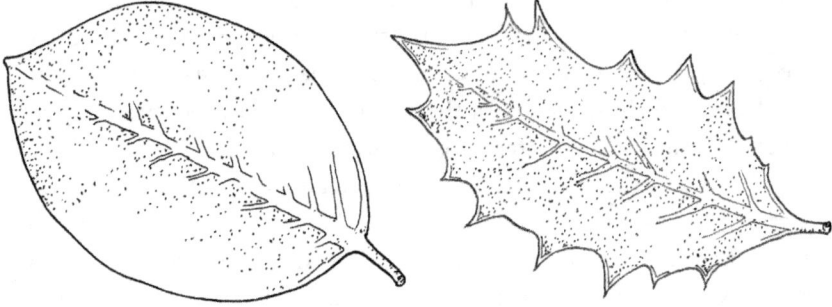

HOLLY (*ILEX AQUIFOLIUM*) is a familiar tree found in woodlands, hedges and more widely. It has a long association with Christmas, largely due to it retaining its perennial, waxy leaves all through the winter and producing red berries around the year's turn. In fact, in pre-Victorian times 'Christmas trees' meant holly bushes.

Holly is also associated with a host of myths and superstitions. In the Christian tradition, the spiny leaves of the holly are associated with Jesus' crown of thorns, and the bright red berries became associated with the shedding of drops of blood. In pre-Christian times, 'The Holly and the Ivy' formed a tradition in which a boy and a girl paraded around a village wearing respectively a suit of each of these evergreens, bringing Nature into the community in the darkest part of the year and welcoming the coming year's fertility.

Bringing holly into the house was also considered to offer protection from malevolent faeries, allowing them shelter in the home without antagonism with the human occupants. There were also taboos against cutting down holly trees, which were frequently left uncut in hedgerows in part in the belief that they obstructed witches that ran along the tops of the hedges.

The leaves of the holly were also useful fodder for livestock when greenery was hard to come by in midwinter, often ground to avoid problems with the pricklier leaves. Holly trees were also often traditionally planted near houses to offer protection from lightning, the tree associated with thunder gods such as Thor and Taranis across Europe.

If some superstitions associated with holly are bizarre, the reality is in many ways even more so. One of the superpowers of the holly is its ability to change form in response to grazing. Unmolested, the leaves of the holly tend to be rounded. However, nibbling by deer, goats and other grazers switches on genes in the plant that make the leaves regrow with sharp spikes. Consequently, the upper leaves of taller holly trees that are out of reach of grazers have smooth edges, whilst the lower leaves grow increasingly prickly in response to the nibbling attentions of various animals.

The holly's defence mechanism is believed to have evolved to protect the tree from excessive grazing by hungry herbivores as well as in response to the attentions of insects, diseases and pathogens. The spiky form of holly leaves, known as 'bristles', are much tougher and more rigid than the smooth leaves and are less nutritious. They are consequently far less readily consumed, enabling the tree to continue to grow and thrive even in areas where grazing pressure is intense.

The genetic material of the holly does not change; this is an epigenetic effect wherein the genes coding for spiky leaves are 'switched on' through environmental factors.

The holly is just one amongst many plant species in which heterophylly (changes in leaf shape triggered by environmental factors) is known to occur. The leaves of various other plants change shape under such environmental factors as submergence or temperature, light level or water availability. The leaf shape of many aquatic plants changes according to whether the leaves are submerged or emergent (above or at the surface). This is seen commonly in rivers and lakes for example in the underwater 'cabbage' leaves of the yellow water lily (*Nuphar lutea*) compared to the floating, rounded waxy leaves seen on the water's surface. Various other water plants, such as various species of water buttercup (*Ranunculus* spp.) and arrowhead (*Sagittaria sagittifolia*), also have differentiated submerged and floating leaves.

In all cases of heterophylly, this adaptive mechanism allows plants to respond rapidly to environmental stimuli, adapting optimally to changes or localised variations through the switching on or off genes yet without fundamental change to the underlying genetic material.

Other epigenetic effects in which shapeshifting is triggered by environmental factors are widespread in nature. The crucian (a fish *Carassius*

carassius) changes body shape in response to chemicals emitted by its predators, making this little potential prey fish harder to engulf and swallow. Variations in the size and mouthparts of some ant species are also responsive to signals from the environment and from chemicals released by the colony. Adaptation of physiology by the three-spined stickleback (*Gasterosteus aculeatus*) in response to salinity, the seasonal development of breeding plumage in birds or colorations and other features in many animals, and changes in form as plants flower or generate fruits are just some amongst many common examples of shapeshifting in nature. Behaviours also 'shapeshift' as environmental factor switch genes on an off in plants and animals.

So, next time you see a holly bush or tree, be aware that you are in the presence of a shapeshifter!

THE LAUGHING YAFFLE

EVERYONE KNOWS THAT frogs go "*Ribbitt, ribbitt*", right? The only problem is that they don't! Of the estimated 4,700 frog species throughout the world, only one – the Pacific tree frog (*Pseudacris regilla*) also known as the Pacific chorus frog – has the well-known "*Ribbitt, ribbitt*" call. (If you have a computer, tablet or smartphone, you can find recordings of the call of this frog by typing in its name.) This small tree frog is widely distributed around the US Pacific Northwest of the US, and is locally the most common frog in river valleys such as those in the Sacramento and Carmel areas. When Hollywood and TV sound engineers wanted frog noises, they went out into the local countryside, overdubbing recorded clips of Pacific tree frogs into movies and television shows situated in Africa, India, Australia, in fact anywhere in the world! And so "*Ribbitt, ribbitt*" is in our lexicon and our perceptions of frog noises globally, even though the vocalisations of these frogs are highly varied – from croaks to "*Haha!*" to duck-like "*Quacks!*" and many more besides – and generally unique to each species.

So too our native woodpeckers.

There are three British species of woodpecker, two commonly seen and heard by the river and the third quite a rarity now. None sound anything like the call of the American cartoon character 'Woody Woodpecker' that tainted our subconscious memories as we grew up!!

The European green woodpecker (*Picus viridis*) also goes by the common name 'yaffle', derived from the loud, laughing call, or 'yaffle' that the bird emits. (Various recordings of the call of the yaffle can be found on the internet.) When flying, green woodpeckers also often emit a noisy ululation, sometimes described phonetically as "*Kyü-kyü-kyück*", particularly when alarmed.

This is a handsome, large bird some 30-36 centimetres (12-14 inches) in length with a wingspan of 45-51 centimetres (18-20 inches). It has a dull green back and pale yellowish-green underside, a yellow rump, and a red crown and nape of the neck. The green woodpecker also has a black 'moustache' stripe, solid black in female birds but with a red centre in the male.

In common with the vocalisations of woodpeckers, the European green woodpecker is also misrepresented in terms of the woodpecking part of its name. Unlike other British woodpecker species, the green woodpecker spends much of its time on the ground where it feeds on ants. Also unlike other British woodpecker species, it rarely 'drums' on trees, and then only as a soft, fast roll in soft wood as its beak is relatively weak. In fact, it barely pecks wood at all!

Green woodpeckers are shy but widely distributed across Europe and into western Asia. They are largely sedentary, remaining loyal all year to preferred habit in which old deciduous trees, in which they nest in holes above ground level, are adjacent to feeding grounds that include grasslands, heaths and orchards containing an abundance of ants. River valleys are a favoured domain, across which the elongated form of the bird can be seen spearing between trees, as well as heard emitting its 'yaffle' call.

In addition to ants, green woodpeckers may also consume other invertebrates as well as, occasionally, small reptiles. A special adaptation that this bird has for its ant-heavy diet – the droppings comprise almost exclusively ant remains – is an exceptionally long tongue (around 10 centimetres or almost 4 inches) that is used to lick up the ants. The tongue is so long relative to the size of the bird's head that it has to be curled around its skull when retracted.

In addition to 'yaffle', many other English folk names relate to the laughing call including, for example, laughing Betsey, yaffingale, laughing bird, yappingale, yuckel and Jack Eikle. For some, the green woodpecker has an ability to bring on rain, reflected in folk names including rain-bird, weather cock and wet bird.

The green woodpecker may be doubly misrepresented, both in terms of popular misconception of its call as well as being saddled with a name that does not reflect its habit. However, this elegant bird is a reasonably common sight in river valleys and when feeding in gardens and on grasslands, parkland and other ant-rich habitats. It is always a welcome 'spot' for the avid river-watcher year-round, and its 'yaffle' cry is an enrichment.

REALISING THE NATURE OF NATURE

IN LIFE, WE often have to seek out the silver linings of dark clouds. One such silver lining from the Covid-19 experience has been how people – not just twitchers, botanisers, bug-hunters, fishermen and others closer to biodiversity but all of us – have found solace, sanity and a greater affinity with nature.

Friends from Jaipur in the Indian state of Rajasthan told me how the city had fallen silent, the traffic fumes clearing, with birdsong filling the city as birds re-established themselves in an urban environment from which daily bustle and pollution had formerly driven them away. Another friend in Bologna, Italy, sent me videos of deer and wild boar passing by his city-centre house. Similar tales emerged around the world. Locked down and with mounting 'cabin fever', many more people took local exercise in green and pleasant surroundings, rediscovering a countryside or spaces they had largely taken for granted.

The past centuries of human development, particularly since the European Industrial Revolution, have increasingly divorced us from nature. We in the richer, developed world now largely take food for granted, procuring it mainly from retailers served by international supply chains insulating our awareness of the soils and cultures from which it was produced. So too water, that comes from the tap and vanishes down the plug hole, with little thought about the natural systems that produce, resorb and purify it. Our consumption and awareness of sources of energy is similar.

Even much of our entertainment is 'canned' rather than experiential. Much though I appreciate nature programmes on the television, it is too easy to simply 'consume' them divorced from the immersive experience of the natural world with all its shifting seasonality, aromas, colours and textures, but also its vulnerability and dwindling vitality.

Today, we are substantially insulated from the 'real world': the underpinning if largely unseen biotic world that regenerates the air we breathe, the water we drink, the food we eat and that regulates flood and drought, climate and air quality, providing us also with cultural richness. We are also as equally insulated from the harsh realities of the massive degradation that our growing population and lifestyle demands have already imposed upon, and continue to suppress, its integrity, resilience and capacities to bear our weight into the future.

The policy world, globally as well as nationally, is slowly waking up to the dangers of lifestyle demands divorced from, but overwhelmingly dependent upon, nature's regulating, renewing, healing and supporting processes.

The language of 'nature-based solutions' is increasingly prevalent. This includes, for example, 'natural flood management' solutions, such as allowing water to be retained and buffered upstream in floodplains rather than artificially drained from them exacerbating flood surges downstream. It is also in the language of urban development, for example as 'green infrastructure'. This includes SuDS: 'sustainable drainage systems' that use or emulate natural hydrological processes rather than being solely reliant on pipework. There is also renewed interest in the roles of urban trees in buffering noise, visual and storm intensity and attenuating poor air quality as well as storm water. So too the cooling, aesthetic and health-related benefits of urban greenspaces.

Increasing numbers of medical practices are prescribing 'green exercise' to address various aspects of mental and physical health. Wetland systems installed for flood management and the treatment of pollutants are also gaining traction. In our food systems, there is renewed interest in the foundational role of living, biologically active soils, as we face food sufficiency challenges and the threat of input-intensive farming not only exhausting the productivity of soils treated as inert media dependent upon fertilisers and pesticides but further excluding the world's poorest from the benefits of declining harvests.

At the most basic biological as well as other levels, we cannot live without nature. Linked policy areas are slow to catch up with recognition of this fundamental reality, and the potentially dire consequences for continuing human security and opportunity if ecological degradation is not seriously addressed.

So, long may the 'silver lining' of greater awareness of the healing and tranquillity of nature last. However, 'business as usual' has a nasty habit of making us forget our holidays, breaks and calmness through a de-stressed life that puts us into closer connection with surrounding ecosystems and communities, as 'normal life' reimposes its pressures upon us.

The recent reawakening of the pandemic has been a generational (and we hope no more frequent) turning point for us to challenge former established norms, and to seek a 'new normal' that values the tangible, spiritual, health, economic and other benefits of lifestyles reflecting and conserving the central role that natural systems play in our lives.

As we progress through the United Nations' *Decade on Ecosystem Restoration* (2021-2030) and beyond it, it is incumbent upon us all to play our part in restoring nature and its processes to their place at the regenerative heart of all our interests.

THE FUNGAL
INTERNET

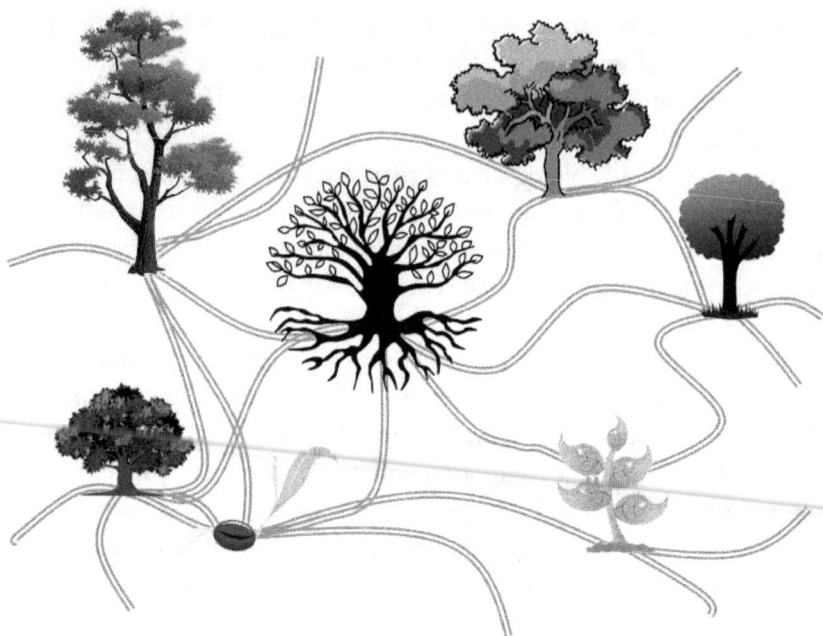

WE ALL KNOW what fungi are and what they do, right? Toadstools, mushrooms and brackets on trees – some edible and some poisonous – betray their presence, as they feed off decaying matter. That much is true, but they do so much more besides.

In fact, the visible fruiting bodies – those toadstools, mushrooms and brackets growing from tree trunks and logs pushed up ephemerally into the air above the ground or decaying organic matter to release spores to spread the species – comprise only a minuscule proportion of fungal biomass.

The primary constituents of fungal organisms are microscopic tubular hyphae. Whilst individual hyphal filaments are typically only 4-6 microns (μm) in diameter, and therefore invisible to the human eye, they comprise the vast bulk of fungal biomass out of sight and out of mind below the surface.

A network of long, tubular hyphae is collectively known as a 'mycelium', and the cumulative mass of a mycelium can be gigantic. One fungal species, *Armillaria ostoyae*, common in cooler regions of the northern hemisphere, claims the record as the world's largest known single organism by area. A mycelium of this fungal species in the Strawberry Mountains of eastern Oregon in the United States was found to span an area of 3.5 square miles (2,200 acres or 9.1 km²), estimated to be 8,000 years old and to weight up to 35,000 tons.

Fungal hyphae extend out into soils and organic matter, reaching out to new food sources upon which they release enzymes, which are technically known as 'exoenzymes' as they are released outside rather than inside the hyphae. Nutrients and minerals released through the action of exoenzymes are absorbed by the hyphae, and distributed to feed the wider mycelium.

In the main, fungi are saprophytes, breaking down and living off dead organic matter. However, some fungi are parasitic and may be causative agents of disease. Other fungal species have evolved ingenious mechanisms to trap and digest nematodes (small worms). Most though exhibit a diversity of metabolic pathways, enabling them to break down a range of organic matter. They thereby play important roles in maintain the cycling of chemicals in the environment, including converting them into forms more readily available to plants. In fact, at least 90% of land plants – possibly all of them – are in mutually-beneficial relationships with fungi that grow within and around their roots. This relationship is defined by the term 'mycorrhiza', with sugars and other organic matter manufactured by the plants exchanged for soil nutrients, minerals and water liberated by the fungi. This direct interrelationship may be vital for the success of the host plant, which is less able or indeed unable to access these nutrients without the symbiotic agency of fungi and other microorganisms within the rhizosphere.

The diverse capacities of fungi to chemically recycle matter can be useful when it comes to treating land contaminated by such problematic pollutants are diesel oil, as some fungi can adapt their chemical armoury to break down these and other problematic organic contaminants.

Fungi play another surprising role. Amazingly, they act as a sub-soil 'internet'. Long hyphae connect the roots of trees, bushes and other plants across broad landscapes. This fungal internet can also share nutrients between plants. One study in America in 1997 demonstrated that two tree species, Douglas fir and paper birch, can transfer and exchange carbon via their sub-soil fungal connection. Other research has since shown that different plants can exchange nitrogen and phosphorus by this same route. It is conjectured that larger trees may 'help out' smaller trees growing in their shade by sharing nutrients, as the smaller plants are less able to survive without this top-up due to the lack of light in the understory.

Even more amazingly, the fungal internet can also spread messages between plants. Chinese research has shown that, when attacked by harmful microorganisms, plants can release chemical signals into the mycelia that 'warn' neighbouring plants, which are prompted to start producing defensive chemicals. Other studies have found similar chemical communication between plants affected by aphids, the infested plants messaging adjacent plants that are not yet affected.

The fungal mycelium can also be exploited for 'cybercrime'. Some plants, like the parasitic phantom orchid (*Cephalanthera austiniae*: its common name reflecting its lack of photosynthetic pigments), use the hyphal network to 'steal' carbon from other plants.

Another function performed by the fungal internet is that it can be used to dissuade unwelcome plants. Plants such as eucalyptus trees and marigolds are known to be allelopathic, releasing chemicals that inhibit the growth of other competitor plants. Mycelia have also been found to spread these toxic chemicals into surrounding soils.

The term 'wood wide web' is increasingly being used to describe communication services provided by fungi to plants and other organisms.

You may have seen the blockbuster movie *Avatar*, released in 2009 and produced by James Cameron, where all living things are connected by unseen connections below the surface of the forest soil. Fanciful perhaps but, we are learning, maybe closer to the truth of how plants are far more highly interactive via this fungal information and chemical superhighway than we formerly assumed.

WEIR-ED

WE ARE SO used to a British riverscape of weirs, narrow bridges with falls, 'dark satanic mills', dams and other built structures that we don't perhaps stop often enough to ask why these impoundments are there and what they do to a river system. Closer examination reveals how weir-ed, or just plain weird, the rivers of Britain and Europe are relative to their natural state.

A study published in December 2020 in the prestigious scientific journal *Nature* identified 1.2 million instream barriers in 36 European countries, constituting 0.74 barriers per kilometre of river. The greatest barrier densities occurred in the heavily modified rivers of central Europe, and the lowest in remote, sparsely populated alpine areas. Some relatively unfragmented rivers are still found in the Balkans, the Baltic states and parts of Scandinavia and southern Europe, albeit that many are under pressure from proposed dam schemes.

Does this matter and, if so, why?

Rivers support some of Earth's richest biodiversity, adapted to conditions that include free movement up and down river systems as well as across river channels and into floodplains and other riparian hinterlands. Most obviously, any obstruction in the channel has significant implications for migratory fishes such as salmon, trout, eels, shad and the shorter spawning migrations made by many other species. In other countries, we can add river dolphins, freshwater turtles and a host of other organisms.

Obstructions to the free flow of water also alter the movement of suspended matter. Large dams trap between 90 and 100% of the sediment passing through them. A significant consequence of this is seen in microcosm when looking upstream and then downstream of any weir or narrow bridge on home soil. Upstream, you will observe a stiller, muddier reach as currents are retarded, allowing fine suspended matter to drop out in backwaters. Downstream, the water rushes over the weir stripped of its burden of suspended sediment, creating a pool of eroded gravels and retreating banks no longer nourished by that load of organic, mineral and other matter. At grander scale, major dams result in massive downstream erosion and nutrient starvation in the corridors and deltas of large rivers, with major structural, food security and economic consequences for people dependent upon them.

Habitat modification differentially affects the suitability of rivers for different species of organisms. There are winners, such as exposure of gravels in the tails of weirs often favouring gravel-spawning fishes such as trout, barbel, chub, grayling and dace. These riffles also support the needs of water plants such as *Ranunculus* (water buttercups), the sinuous tresses of which prosper in streamy and turbulent water that dislodges algae that might otherwise smother them in slack flows. But there are also losers, including many plant species (including *Ranunculus* amongst others) that are smothered out by a rain of fine silt and algal growth in stiller reaches, with 'weedy' vegetation displacing naturally more diverse botanical assemblages and their associated fauna.

It is not just wildlife that suffers from the impacts of familiar and sometimes culturally important 'dark satanic mills' and other relics of former industries and river management, or of new impoundments such as large dams designed with a myopic view concerning their net value and sustainability. So too do the many human benefits that flow from naturally broad riverine biodiversity, including plants and animals exploited for their food, medicinal, craft, recreational, aesthetic and other uses. The many natural processes of free-flowing river systems also degrade when channels are constrained, rendering them less able to buffer flows and so deepening risks of both floods and droughts. Diversity and functionality of habitats that support natural water and air purification, soil fertilisation, nutrient transformation, carbon cycling and other important processes are also depleted.

Culturally, we may like fishing, bathing, sitting by or otherwise enjoying the rush of water over a weir. But, from the perspectives of the natural state and the range of benefits to society provided by river systems, these man-made obstructions to the free flow of water, sediment and biota are just plain weird... or should that be weir-ed?

JANUARY

GLORIOUS MONOCHROME

W HEN DAYLIGHT IS at its most muted and brief, as the sun traces its lowest and shortest arc across the cool winter sky, it may seem that colour has seeped from the landscape. This is no more so than under a lowering, slate-grey blanket of cloud. Light and colour, it seems, drain interminably from the world. It is then no wonder that our forebears greeted with palpable relief the sun's perceptible rebound in the days following the solstice, a cause for celebration that the nadir of the then-known universe had been passed.

This is the time when leaves are fully, or at least mainly, shed, rendering deciduous trees down to their dark skeletons. Riverbanks too are razed back to bare earth, former vivid hues largely muted to mere textures. Nature at its lowest ebb may, ostensibly, seem no more than a scaffold of bones, robbed of soft form and vibrancy.

But, look again, and all is richly toned. Just as a finely framed black-and-white photograph conjures in the mind a rich kaleidoscope of the most vibrant energies, contrasts and textures, the silhouettes of nature too tell technicolour tales of form and function moulded by powerful natural processes.

Nature at this time is, though visually pared back to its most essential forms, so much more than a toneless residue. Trees bereft of greenery are revealed as architectural works of art, each species so distinctive in its exquisite moulding of structure to function with any two of the same type uniquely crafted and no mere facsimile.

Though of a more limited palate, cloudscapes too reveal a broad and ever-shifting spectrum of grey tones. Bankside soils, sand, shingle, gravels and silt may traverse a narrow range of subdued browns and greys yet, in their texture and diversity, tell tales of the scour of currents and accretion in slacks, pregnant with the life they harbour readying itself for explosive release in the forthcoming spring.

As clouds part on a chill winter night, frost-dried air reveals, at its most sparklingly brilliant, the monochrome vista of ink-black space dotted with countless stars. Constellations peer back at the observer, as they have at countless generations of stargazers throughout human history and beyond that into the depths of prehistory. Untold generations have read into the night's monochrome tableau the most lurid and highly coloured tales of beasts and hunters, myths, Gods and the struggles between them.

Musical notes, apparently little more than black dots on staves printed on white paper, bear to the musician cascades of emotion from soaring elation to the deepest despair. Letters and words printed on a page also have no need of coloured fonts to evoke in the reader a kaleidoscope of emotions from awe and wonder, to fear, love or empathy. The best books, as we know, are better than film adaptations for the vivid images that we project within the cinema of our mind. So too, the skilled musician will, through their interpretation of weave of those little black dots on the stave, reveal multi-hued emotions hidden to many who have played them before.

In its most monochrome of seasons, nature too is a parchment vivid in its storytelling of life at pause, shaped by insuperable forces to embody what has been and what is to come.

Life in monochrome is never more vivid.

WHERE DOES NATURE LIVE?

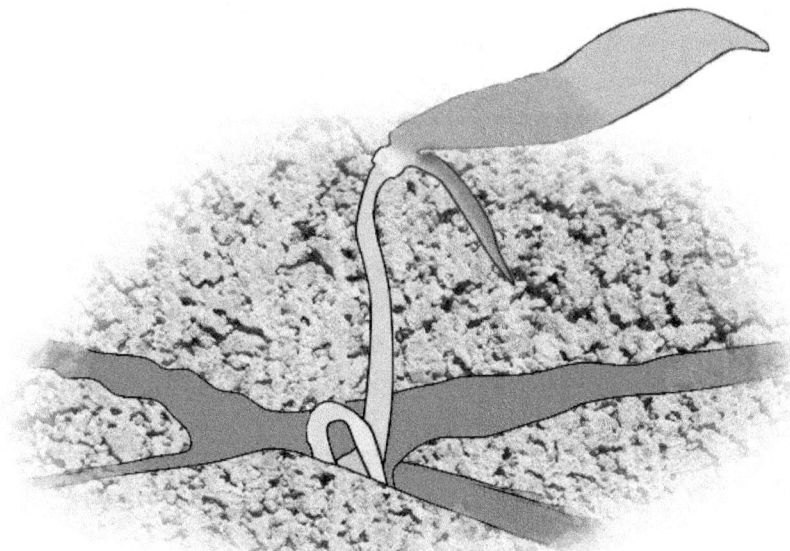

HAVE YOU EVER stopped to ponder where nature lives? This may seem like a naïve question, but it is one that really matters. It cuts to deeper issues of what nature actually is and, indeed, our relationship with it.

Common perceptions might be that nature is out there in the countryside; something we go to visit from our settlements. But the reality is that much of 'the countryside' is seriously depleted in wildlife due to intensification of land uses that have been a major factor in making the UK one of the most nature-depleted countries on this planet.

Green and pleasant land? Green maybe, but tidied and treated to an inch of its life to rid pests and diseases with collateral damage to wild plants and animals. For example, the 2023 'State of Nature' report developed and published as a collaboration between the wide range of conservation and research organisations found that the abundance of 753 terrestrial and freshwater species has on average fallen by 19% across the UK since 1970, including 290 species (38%) that had declined in abundance and 205 species (27%) had increased. The UK distributions of 4,979 invertebrate species had also, on average, decreased by 13% since 1970. A 2022 study led by Butterfly Conservation found that 80% of butterfly species in the UK had declined since 1976, with this decline particularly pronounced in grassland butterflies amongst which 90% of species showed a decrease. Likewise, a 2021 'The State of Britain's Wildflowers' report published by The Botanical Society of Britain and Ireland found that wildflower meadows are not only now a rare habitat in the UK but that wildflowers have declined by about 97% since the 1930s, with alarming rates of decline in recent decades that the report's authors branded as a "national scandal" requiring urgent action.

All this alarmism is not a dig at farmers. It is the wider market forces we have instituted across society that drives intensive methods focused on maximised output at any cost. It is these wider pressures that reflect society-wide misunderstanding of the natural world and effective disregard of its vital importance for our co-existence with it.

Co-existence is not merely 'nice to have', a net cost on the things we do, but reflects that natural cycles and processes that cleanse and regenerate air, water and fertile soils. They naturally buffer against flooding and drought as well as pest and disease outbreaks of stock and humans. For example, Covid-19 and other of a range of 'zoonotic' diseases jumping from animals to humans are facilitated by degradation of the 'firewalls' presented by complex yet now diminished ecosystems. Nature inspires and enriches, defines the places in which we live or otherwise enjoy, builds soil structure, hosts pollinators, generates useful resources such as wood and artistic resources, and yields many more benefits besides.

A green but increasingly sanitised landscape is pleasant to whom, exactly? Because depletion of nature degrades our security and life opportunities.

The same rubrics apply in the settlements in which we live. Nature is not magically segregated by anthropocentric labels such as 'rural' versus 'urban'. In fact, much of nature is highly adapted to built environments, as for example the ways in which swallows and house martins have learned to nest in the 'cliff faces' of our houses, blackbirds and robins clear pests from our gardens, and peregrine falcons hunt from and nest in the tall structures we have created. Our garden ponds present a vital network of habitats for newts and frogs hemmed in by increasingly drained and converted hinterlands, and present 'stepping stones' for birds and small mammals in transit.

Hedgerows, verges and green spaces provide corridors for wildlife to establish and move amongst us. This is just one of the reasons why they should be valued and carefully managed to bring those many services that nature supplies – benefits flowing to society that we have inadvertently but meticulously razed from 'the countryside' – into the heart of the places we live. Rachel Carson's seminal 1962 book *Silent Spring* may have been principally a prescient warning about cavalier use of persistent pesticides, but could equally be a metaphor for the strangulation of life-giving and inspiring nature from the places we inhabit.

Nature, with all its complexity and richness, generating purifying, regulating and inspirational gifts to humanity, is inherently diverse and chaotic (in its true scientific and positive sense). An aggressively tidy-minded approach rids our homes of the richness of birdsong, splashes of floral colour and rich aromas, educational and inspirational sights and senses, natural buffers to noise and flood, and communal areas characterised by pleasant surroundings.

Turning the green spaces and verges within our habitations into 'bowling greens' is like painting over every picture in an art gallery with magnolia emulsion, drowning out beautiful music with monotone, or banning literature in favour of a 'party manifesto'.

Overly 'tidy' greenery is a poor place in which to live; we need to learn to love nature in every place around us, and to value all the things it does to bear, brighten and broaden our lives.

POOLED RESOURCES

S HEETS OF WATER lying across the landscape after heavy rainfall can often elicit panicky reactions amongst many in the population. We are raised to expect 'dry land' to be entirely distinct from the open waters of lakes and rivers, and to expect water to stay obediently within the spaces we allot to it.

This expectation of separation was not, however, the norm a century and more ago. The natural state of the landscape is one of progressive transition rather than stark division between wet and dry. Drainage of the British and northern European landscape has a long history, evidentially pre-Roman though substantially ramped up during Roman occupation. Land drainage accelerated with gusto throughout medieval and post-medieval ages under successive waves of 'agricultural improvement' that largely regarded wetlands as wasteful. Successive waves of legally founded 'enclosure' saw huge swathes of land, formerly constituting commons supporting the livelihoods of the bulk of the population, annexed as private property held by privileged people and generally converted for the narrow purpose of boosting crop production and profitability.

The 'green and pleasant lands' we know and inhabit today are a legacy of serial legally sanctioned dispossession of the masses, privatised and drained for the pursuit of private profit.

Fenland, in the east of England, is the 'best' example of widespread worst practice, a grim accolade with drainage of Yorkshire's long-forgotten fenlands running it close. Progressive drainage of the Fens dates back at least to Roman earthworks and dykes, later progressed by Saxon monks amongst others, and most famously extended in the years either side of the English Civil War – one wave beforehand (1630 to 1637) and another after is cessation (1650 to 1652) – in the form of major earthwork, channelisation and bypass programmes massively draining the 1,500 square miles or so of formerly extensive marsh in a landscape that was neither fully aquatic or terrestrial. The war shifted from opposing human ideologies to aggressive subjugation of nature favouring the rich new owners of annexed land and, with it, sweeping away the rights and livelihoods of the many landless inhabitants and communities that has subsisted on reeds and fish, waterfowl and peat, and other of the fens' rich resources from time immemorial. Today, true fens are a rarity in Fenland with only tiny and fragmented remnants spanning 254.5 hectares (less than 1,000th of the area of the once-extensive fens).

Following the threat of food deficiency during the Second World War years, alleviated by convoys vulnerable to enemy action, domestic food sufficiency became an overriding political priority resulting in subsidisation of mass drainage and profound change to the national landscape. In this post-war era, water became a new enemy to be rushed off the land and out to sea as quickly as possible.

Today, we live within a desiccated legacy that, through lifelong familiarity, we regard as normal and natural however divorced it may be from the native state. Water lying for any time in the landscape became the rarity that it remains today.

Does this matter? Well, yes because, as increasing incidences of drought under a changing climate and the spiralling thirst of a rising human population demonstrate to us, water is one of our most vital assets that we rush out to sea at our collective peril. Better to allow it to reside in the landscape – literally a pooled resource – slowly to percolate into the soil and replenish serially over-abstracted and depleted aquifers that also feed perennial river flows. Beyond this utilitarian argument for allowing moisture back into our landscapes, many organisms – wildfowl, fish such as burbot, wetland plants, the insects that depend upon them and many more vital for natural cycles of chemicals and energy, pollination and pest regulation – depend upon the very wetted or naturally moist environments we have expunged. Retained moisture is also vital for myriad natural processes that store carbon, helping us address climate change. Additional wetland processes recycle nutrients and other substances, turning wastes into resources. Wetted land also rebuilds soil that we currently desiccate and till, resulting in massive loss and degradation. And they regulate both flooding and drought, and enhance the vitality and functions of soil organisms upon which our continued wellbeing depends.

Perhaps counterintuitively, water pooled on landscapes substantially reduces threats to residences and infrastructure as, if not detained and slowed, it would be rushing off in concentrated, mucky spates causing much more damage and threat of flooding. The more water we see on the land, the less it can harm us and the more benefits it can confer.

We drain land to maximise supplies of food – no one is going to argue that food sufficiency is not important – but land drainage supports only a particular narrow, inherited model of intensive food production. Naturally enriched grazing and many other traditional and emerging nature-friendly farming systems are actively enhanced by restored landscape hydrology.

Pooling watery assets makes so much sense in these wider contexts, rather than fighting against the very natural processes sustaining out continuing wellbeing. We just need to think differently, and to realise and act upon the inherent value of natural resources of all kinds.

SMALL BUT POWERFUL

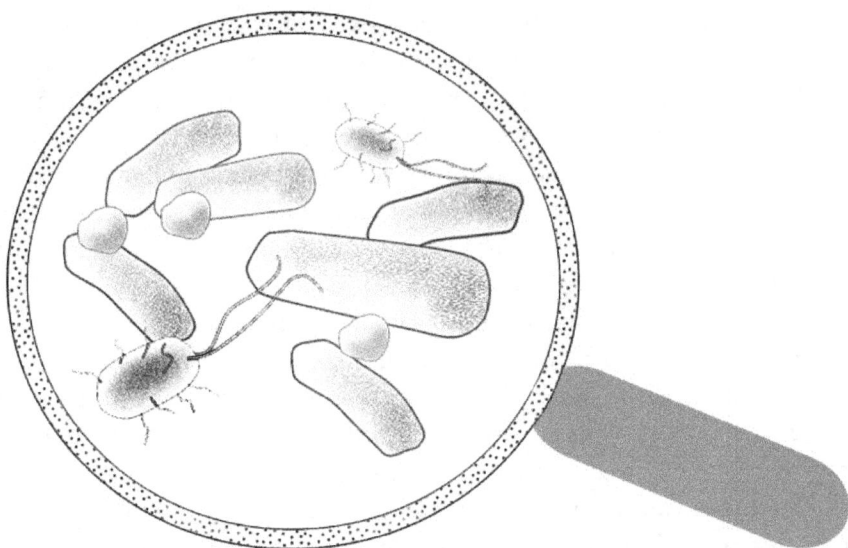

H AVE YOU EVER considered or played guessing games with others about what may be the most important living things in the riverine and wider landscape?

Is it the top predators: larger and more charismatic creatures such as otters, badgers, herons and sparrowhawks that consume and shape the population structure of the wider fauna of the river system? Or, at the other end of the scale, is it the plants: algae, grasses, herbs, shrubs and trees that capture the sun's radiation, forming the base of food chains? What about the myriad invertebrates that consume, 'clean up' and transform plant and other organic matter into living animal tissues and energetic biochemicals making all that solar energy available to other organisms? Or maybe it is the fish that serve as intermediate links in food chains, and that transport nutrients around ecosystems as they eat, migrate and excrete?

We may all have our favourite riverine life forms, whether we are by persuasion botanists or anglers, otter-watchers or entomologists. But the flaw in thinking about a 'most important' is, of course, that all these lives are so interconnected and interdependent that they are all greatly important whether large or small, colourful or dull, loved or unknown, or producer, consumer or decomposer. Take one brick out of this elaborate construction and the whole edifice collapses.

Of massive importance though is the vastly greater diversity of largely unidentified and commonly overlooked microscopic organisms inhabiting all niches throughout planetary ecosystems. These tiny and bewilderingly varied life forms are in reality the overwhelmingly dominant players in the complex biogeochemical and energetic cycles upon which all other life depends. We could lose all visible living organisms and, though impoverished, this world would continue albeit in much-changed form. But lose all that life invisible to the naked human eye, and the visible ecosystem would simply spiral down into immediate collapse.

From cycles of carbon and nitrogen, phosphorus and silicon, metals of many types and organic molecules, it is the microbial world that does the vast majority of the legwork. Larger beasts and plants are, at best, bit-part players. Humanity, with all our sense of self-importance, is in a natural state so minimal as to be inherently inconsequential.

Inherently inconsequential, yet far from that in terms of the consequences of the ways in which we humans live our lives today. In fact, the cumulative disruption of these vital natural cycles through our lifestyle demands and unconstrained economic activities threatens to destabilise and overturn the whole applecart of the otherwise self-sustaining biospheric system.

We, in short, need the humility to see ourselves not as most important in the workings of the living planet, but on a par with microbes and other organisms from which we may learn how to live more harmoniously in synergy with the resilient yet vulnerable machinery of nature upon which our prospects for living healthy, prosperous, secure and fulfilled lives utterly depends.

Nature can thrive in our absence, but we are wholly dependent upon the tiny life forms of which we may be barely or entirely aware.

Out of sight, out of mind, yet small and powerful and deserving of our profound respect.

SCENTS OF THE SEASONS

I T IS MAGICAL to be out in the countryside in the calm hours before dawn, be that by the river or walking the quiet lanes.

The still air bears a richness of scents. Whilst our eyes perceive little more than silhouettes and a limited palette of greys, the aromas of living nature are brought to the fore through greater awareness of what our olfactory sensitivity is telling us about our surroundings when half-light denies us our generally primary reliance on vision.

Full daylight rewards the eyes with a bewildering spectrum of greens, let alone the variety of other colours, and ears connect us with a full orchestra of vocalisations and rustlings. But, in these quieter, darker hours before the human world is busy and the eyes are less discerning, the breadth and variety of nature's aromas present themselves, cycling with the seasons.

Early springtime brings us a heady tang of ramsons – wild garlic – sufficing the air with a pungency as strident as the yelp of a vixen.

As the days lengthen, meadow grasses raise their spikes ever higher, the scent of vernal grass adding a sweet note to the dawn air. As daylight intrudes further into the earlier hours, fragrant notes of flowers opening add their textures as they lure in pollinating insects.

As buds unfurl and new leaves fan out in the hedgerows and from riparian and other trees, there is a waxiness, amplified at encroaching dusk on still evenings.

And, when the hay is cut, first we enjoy the smell of new-mown grass and, later as the hay is left to dry in windrows or baled ready for collection, a characteristic half-sweet, half-musty aroma suffuses the air space.

By then, hemlock plants will have raised themselves from the riverbank, thrusting upwards to present their umbels to the warming sky and emanating a mustiness not so different from the trail of a dog fox.

Near the wooded margins and from the hedgerows, honeyed wafts of honeysuckle greet us by dusk and dawn, an olfactory siren call to moths.

To the tuned nose, the approach of summer showers is signalled by a tangible iron tang in the air. When the rain comes, it brings with it an aroma with freshness, cleanness and wetness beloved by many people. And after the rain has fallen, particularly after a storm, there is another distinctive, slightly sweet and sharp smell all of its own. This distinctive smell has a name, the term 'petrichor' coined in 1964 as a synthesis of the Greek terms 'petra' (meaning 'stone') and 'ichor' (a special substance that flows in the veins of gods). The petrichlor aroma is created by a melange of plant oils, bacteria and ozone, generated by the falling rain and thrown up by its impact on the soil.

The seasons turn still. With declining day length, mustier tones of vegetation emanate once it is sent from its summer functions. In darker recesses, accumulating leaf litter adds rich, earthy notes to the sweetly and mildly alcoholic waft of fallen fruit.

The languid river before the arrival of winter spates and the dewy moisture on vegetation also enriches the bankside with its dank and rich flavours.

Foxes are by now more active, their passage leaving a wake of fusty aromas that linger as a calling card that this is their domain. The tang of burnt leaves lingers in stiller air.

Soon, the sweetly musty odour of silage broken out for livestock pervades the still dawn air along with the earthy, warm breath of cattle and the tang of moist trampled soil tinged with their urine around feeding stations.

As the days chill down and the leaves have fallen, frosts clarify the early morning leaving a sense on the nose not merely of cold but of cleanliness and a clean slate as the seasonal cycle turns once again.

For such a rich sense, it is surprising how the adjectival lexicon for smell is so much narrower than that for sight. This, of course, is a human-centred view of the world, primarily reflecting that we are primarily visual creatures. Foxes, cats and many other creatures abroad in the dark hours navigate a wholly different sensory landscape. If they, or indeed African elephants that have the strongest sense of smell in the animal kingdom, used adjectives in the ways we do then how much richer would the language of smells be?

FEBRUARY

FROZEN WASTELAND?

W AKING UP WITH condensation on the windows, emerging with
trepidation into frigid air from under the warm embrace of the
duvet, donning clothes to creep cautiously out onto a slippery path to scrape
frost from the car windscreen, swaddling ourselves in layers of unflattering
garments as armour against the chill... a cold snap is not always hugely
welcome. But it is far from all bad!

Rather, an arctic spell is one of the characteristic features of living in an
inherently variable temperate climate. Akin to the experiences of many people
who have spent an extended time living in other climatic zones, I used to miss
the shift of seasons as well as the day-to-day unpredictability of the weather.
Winter conditions are just one swatch of hues in the rich meteorological and
environmental kaleidoscope that characterises our location and time on this
planet. Under a fast-changing climate, our experiences over successive warmer
years might lead us to forget what harder winter weather is all about, though
those of us who recall the winter of 1963 will forever have it imprinted in our
minds. But our experience of winter is integral to what makes us and our
geographical place distinct.

Our wonderfully diverse ecosystems are a product of millions of years of
adaptive response to local environmental conditions and variability. Nature's

marvellously intricate adaptations – of plants to set seeds and develop
overwintering buds or tubers, of birds to migrate away to warmer climates
or to arrive here to escape more hostile conditions in their summer breeding
ranges, of insects to find shelter or to pupate or hibernate – are all part of our
regionally distinctive natural character in which winter is a key trigger.

A world without sticky buds, skeletal trees silhouetting the horizon,
dusk-time murmurations of starlings, cool mist hugging the sward of river
valley meadows at dawn, or the influx of fieldfares as we head into the 'bleak
midwinter' would be a poorer place.

Nature's adaptations gift us seasonal joys such as kicking through fallen
leaves on late-autumnal and winter walks, the spectacle of deep-hued sloes
and vivid rosehips and hawes in hedgerows, and the seasonal recipes, folk
medicines and folklore linked to that natural response to the seasons. And,
of course, those snow-drifted landscapes, holly and robins that feature on
Christmas cards – oddly enough also in cards sold in many countries where
those species do not occur and that do not experience seasonal snow! – along
with the heady aroma of roasting chestnuts and wood smoke. The colder
months imbue us with so many cultural riches.

Although the seasonal cold causes a diapause in the life cycles of many
familiar facets of our wildlife, it is also a powerful control on the proliferation
of potential pest animals, weeds and microbes. Without that seasonal reset,
we could well be over-run.

A winterscape is no frozen wasteland: it is a winter wonderland of huge
environmental and cultural wealth. It is also the resistance against which
nature's life force builds tension, like a wound clock, as seeds, bulbs, eggs, buds,
pupae and many more living forms are held seasonally in check, awaiting the
trigger of lengthening days to explode into fullness as winter loosens its grip.

THE SWIFT ASSASSIN

T HE SWIFT FLIGHT of a sparrowhawk strafing scrub and hedge lines to intercept unwary feathered prey is a dramatic winter sight.

The Eurasian sparrowhawk (*Accipiter nisus*), also known as the northern sparrowhawk, is one of our smaller native birds of prey with a wingspan of up to 55-70 centimetres (22-27 inches). Female hawks, up to 25% larger than adult males, are about the size of a feral pigeon and are overall brownish in colour and distinguished by horizontal bars on the greyish breast feathers and a greyer back and wings. Male birds have bluish-grey back and wings and orangey-brown bars on their chest and belly. Both adult birds have bright yellow or orangey eyes, long yellow legs, long talons and reddish cheeks. By contrast, immature sparrowhawks of under a year old have brown wings and backs, with chestnut-brown edges to the feathers.

Its rounded wings and relatively long, narrow tail elegantly adapts the sparrowhawk for hunting smaller songbirds in confined spaces, such as in dense woodland. Gardens and parkland too provide ideal hunting grounds, adapting these birds to towns and cities as well as rural areas. Sparrowhawks are distributed throughout the British Isles except for parts of the Scottish Highlands, the Western Isles and Shetland. Beyond the British Isles, sparrowhawks have a wide geographical range across Europe and Asia spanning as far as Siberia and Japan in the east. In some of these regions, sparrowhawks are migratory, some even overwintering in East Africa.

Sparrowhawks predominantly hunt small birds such as finches, sparrows and tits. However, larger female hawks can tackle bigger prey such as thrushes, starlings and pigeons. 120 different bird species have been recorded as prey, and some sparrowhawks are also known to catch bats. Sometimes they ambush their prey from a perch, though mainly they 'strafe' hedge and woodland margins, flying low and often suddenly changing direction to surprise their prey. The alarm calls of small prey species signal the presence of sparrowhawks, alerting other birds to danger.

Sparrowhawks breed in woodland, building nests up to 60 centimetres (2 feet) across using twigs. Females lay four or five pale blue, brown-spotted eggs. Breeding success depends on diet, the male bird bringing food to the female whilst she broods the eggs. Chicks hatch after 33 days and fledge after a further 24 to 28 days. A typical sparrowhawk lifespan is four years.

The fortunes of sparrowhawks in the British Isles have varied at the hands of humanity. Numbers were stable until the 1800s. However, from the Victorian era, the species went into decline through persecution at the hands of gamekeepers and Victorian trophy hunters. The decline was sustained until the Second World War when, with people more focused on killing perceived human enemies than wild animals, sparrowhawk numbers began to recover. All was well until the widespread introduction and use of organochlorine pesticides such as DDT from the 1950s, which had a devastating effect on top predators as pesticides were 'biomagnified' along food chains. Due to such symptoms as the thinning of eggshells and reduced breeding success, sparrowhawk numbers crashed across the British Isles from the late 1950s, almost disappearing entirely from eastern England where pesticides were used most intensively.

Sparrowhawk populations have recovered more recently with the progressive banning of the most problematic pesticides, mirroring rebounding numbers of buzzards, kestrels and red kites. However, wider pressures leading to declining prey species are again suppressing numbers of predatory species.

There are lingering concerns in the minds of some people that sparrowhawks predate too heavily on small birds threatening their survival. The reality is that sparrowhawks and songbirds have co-evolved and co-existed for millennia. Multi-decadal scientific research has found that sparrowhawks generally have no or little impact on overall songbird population levels: songbirds were no more common when sparrowhawks were absent than when they were present. All birds require a healthy environment in which to complete their life cycles, and they thrive or decline together. Though formerly often blamed for the loss of racing pigeons, research in Scotland has found that sparrowhawks could account for only 1% of the reported 56% annual loss of these pigeons.

Sparrowhawks have been used in falconry for centuries and, though reputedly hard to tame, are well suited for small quarry such as starlings and blackbirds as well as quail and partridges.

The sparrowhawk, known as *krahui* or *krahug*, also features in Slavic mythology as a sacred bird in Old Bohemian songs. In some parts of England, it was formerly believed that the common cuckoo, for which there is a superficial resemblance and before migration was understood, turned into a Eurasian sparrowhawk in winter. The sparrowhawk was also written about by Alfred, Lord Tennyson in the couplet "*A sparhawk proud did hold in wicked jail, Music's sweet chorister, the Nightingale*".

I never fail to be impressed by the sudden appearance of the silent assassin on the wing by the river.

CELANDINES

A WELL-MEANING VISITOR once started doing some gardening for
us. I caught her weeding out celandines and asked her to stop as my
main interest is in wild plants, not cultivars. She said to me " *You can't have
celandines in a garden!*" Rather than pointing out that is was our garden so
we should chose, I did ask her if she was confident of the difference between
celandines and goldilocks (*Ranunculus auricomus*), another native small
buttercup that I think is wonderful. That put paid to the outbreak of well-
intentioned but misplaced tidiness, with the dispute resolved over a cup of tea!

But I wonder if the celandine – the lesser celandine (*Ficaria verna*),
formerly *Ranunculus ficaria* L., to give it is scientific name and also distinguish
it from the larger and unrelated greater celandine – is perhaps Britain's most
disregarded common plant.

For me, an avid prowler of riverbanks in the year's first quarter, they are
one of the more welcoming symbols of life returning. Even as spate flows in
the river lap the margins, the celandine's fleshy, dark green and heart-shaped

leaves emerge from the soft silt and persist even when inundated for sometimes quite considerable periods.

And then, the flower buds break out into rich and glossy butter-gold blooms, often in carpets, bring welcome summer colour to the banks in the most barren time of year. If not the truest harbinger of spring, then the flower of the celandine is an assuring symbol that the years turn is well progressed and that longer days will soon be upon us. Where they occur in banks in the moist soils that they prefer, the effect can be quite breathtaking and heart-warming. Typically, this can be any time from the end of January into February though, some exceptional years, I have even seen celandine flowers on Boxing Day.

After flowering, celandines rapidly set seed before the above-ground vegetative structure withers. Beneath the soil, the plant's vegetative structure persists, spreading by tubers. These tubers may be further distributed by animals digging into and dispersing the soil.

The early gold of celandine flowers may be welcome to the human eye, but it is more so to insects that are on the wing early in the year as it serves as a rich source of nectar when all else is dormant. The plant's generosity is reciprocated by the pollinating services of visiting insects.

Celandines come and go quickly, flowering and then withering such that they do not impede the growth of plants that sprout and bloom later both in the wild and in the garden.

Celandines are native to central Europe, north Africa and the Caucasus. However, they have been introduced into Iceland and also North America. In America, the plant is known as the fig buttercup and is less welcome as it is considered an invasive species. In fact, several US states have banned the plant, or listed it as a noxious weed, as it is poisonous if ingested raw and potentially fatal to grazing animals. The plant is known to release the toxin protoanemonin when the leaves are wounded, acting naturally as a defence but potentially causing itching, rashes or blistering of the skin, or nausea, vomiting, dizziness, spasms or paralysis when ingested.

Even in Britain, many gardeners regard it as a persistent weed, though it is hard to see what harm this early blooming plant does. There are though a variety of cultivars bred and grown in gardens, reflecting something of a mixed understanding of the plant.

Another common name for the celandine is the pilewort, reflecting a former medicinal use. The tubers are said to resemble piles, and were used by herbalists as a treatment for this affliction. The famous herbalist Nicholas Culpepper (1616-1654) claimed to have treated his daughter for 'scrofula' through use of the celandine. Mesolithic hunter-gatherers in Europe are said to have consumed the plant's roots as a source of carbohydrates boiled, fried or roasted; cooking is known to eliminate its toxicity and celandines have been incorporated in diets as a vegetable or herbal medicine in dried, ground or boiled forms.

William Wordsworth was fond of the celandine, featuring it in three poems: 'To the Small Celandine', 'To the Same Flower' and 'The Small Celandine'. Also C.S. Lewis mentioned celandines in a passage in '*The Lion, the Witch and the Wardrobe*' when Aslan comes to Narnia and the whole wood passes "*...in a few hours or so from January to May*" with "*...wonderful things happening. Coming suddenly round a corner into a glade of silver birch trees Edmund saw the ground covered in all directions with little yellow flowers – celandines*". The humble celandine appears in more literature besides.

Quite why people think that celandines need to be 'controlled' evades me. They are wonderful and much-overlooked native plants bringing joy in the bleakest quarter of the year.

FIRST WORLD
PROBLEMS

S MASHED AVOCADO PAST its use-by date? Supermarket run out of
Prosecco? Fuel prices up again? *"First world problems!"* is a common cry.
    That's a cry I feel with particular weight, having spent much of my
life working across the developing world on natural resource protection or
restoration for the benefit of people and wildlife. Though voiced by some as
if they were existential crises, many first world inconveniences roll off me like
water off a duck's back having seen real resource poverty.
    I hope that my work has benefitted the people with whom I work and
the wider ecosystems that support their needs. But a further benefit from this
experience is a sense of gratitude on returning home and enduring thereafter
when I turn on the tap and the water runs, and when I flush the toilet and
the waste goes away for treatment. Supermarket shelves may occasionally be
sparse when people panic-buy, but there is more than sufficient if one shifts
one's choices. How lucky are we to experience first world problems?
    What are the reasons for this disparity across the world? Accidents
of geography are a significant factor. Extremes of cold and heat, flood and
aridity, are far from evenly distributed globally. Neither are soil productivity,
erodibility and slope steepness. Large expanses of the Earth's surface comprise

highly saline or sodic soils. Any of these factors, in isolation but particularly in combination, restrict food and wider resource and economic security and opportunity.

Another accident of geography provided us in Britain and northern Europe with a local abundance of iron ore and coal. This enabled the birth and rapid spread of industrialisation, generating unprecedented wealth at least for some and with the capacity to invest in education, healthcare and wider economic empowerment. Depletion of the domestic resources fuelling industrialisation then precipitated the European age of empire-building, under which burgeoning business enterprises generated the funds enabling massive land and resource grabs across the undeveloped world.

But unequal resource distribution now cuts deeper than that. As we walk the banks of the river or feel the cool shade of a tree or hedge, we may rightly feel enriched by nature. But do we appreciate that our historic trajectory of industrialisation and land use intensification has led Britain to become one of the most nature-impoverished countries on Earth? Over the past century, Britain has lost over half of its natural habitats, including wetlands and water, forests, grasslands and heathlands. Depletion of our formerly rich legacy of wildlife is compounded by pollution of water, air and water through direct or diffuse inputs from urban, industrial, agricultural and transport sources. Nature's capacities to cleanse and cool air and water, buffer floods, droughts and storms, and to regenerate soil fertility, fisheries and pleasant landscapes is substantially compromised. These pressures are amplified by a changing climate driven by greenhouse gases emitted into the atmosphere disproportionately by the very wealthy nations that pioneered their exploitation and profited most from their promulgation throughout the rest of the planet.

We have formerly offset this massive depletion and degradation of the supportive capacities of our home landscape through the historical accidents of geography that provided us with trading advantages to draw upon global resources at favourable rates, including from less favoured nations. A 2021 UK Food Security Report found that 60% of food consumed in the UK is grown domestically, though actual consumption is closer to 54% when adjusted for exports. We draw even more substantially on global water resources in the form of 'virtual water' consumed to produce imported products such as rice, wheat, cotton, timber and mined materials, cumulatively equivalent to 40% of Britain's total direct water consumption. This international trade in goods with a heavy 'water footprint' has significant geopolitical consequences. Most of this invisible virtual water is effectively exported in exchange for revenue by countries in the Mediterranean, South America and Africa, many of them water-insecure with trade deepening their water security challenges.

The booming global human population and shifting geopolitics now increase competition for dwindling international resources. The historic cocoon of trading advantage that has sustained us in our resource-depleted islands is now unravelling, the illusion of safety supported to date by post-colonial privilege inevitably dissipating. It is long overdue that we look inward to recognise, value, protect and restore the natural resources and processes upon which we will increasingly depend in a rather different future.

First world problems? We have plenty! Protecting or restoring habitats, improving stewardship of our vulnerable and degraded soil, water and other primary resources, better controlling pollution, and reducing overall resource consumption are pressing challenges if we are to secure a sustainable future supported by the foundational resource of a natural world that we have for too long disregarded.

A FLOODPLAIN FOR ALL AGES

IN THE SHORTER days of late winter, much of the natural world is in diapause. But there is a reassurance that we are simply at one of the outer extremities of perpetual natural cycles.

There is equal reassurance that leaves and blooms will swell into early-summer crescendo by June, when nature's annual pendulum swings to the opposite extreme of its arc. And then, with equal certainty, the antipodal gravity of winter will progressively draw it back in months to come. The spring flowers rise and then pass. Summer migrant birds will return to our shores, as will summer migrant butterflies such as the painted lady and clouded yellow, all seeking to propagate as many generations as their life strategies and the British summer can bear.

Daily, the pulse of light and dark, of solar warmth and evening chill, is echoed by the rhythmic opening and closing of many meadow flowers. So too the crepuscular emergence of aquatic insects and the bats that feast upon them, and the changing of the guard from gaudy daytime butterflies to the silent wings of night-flying moths.

From diurnal to seasonal, timespans overlap.

Yet there are far slower tick-tocks at play across the breadth of the floodplain. On the drier lands at the break of slope, overlooking the relative flicker of shorter-term cycles playing out below, tall oak trees germinated from tiny acorns in centuries past have weathered not only storms and floods but also whole human lifetimes, the reigns of monarchs, and radical revolutions in agricultural and industrial practices in the valley below. Even the burgeoning of local villages and towns are the blink of an eye to the slow accretion of rings in the dense wood of their mighty trunks.

Within the river's corridor, the ages-old view of these venerable trees would see generations of junior cousins – ash, hawthorn, blackthorn, alder and willow amongst them – thrust up, reach their magnificent prime, decay and fall back to be subsumed into the alluvial plain. The view of these senior trees would also perceive the serpentine writhing of the river channel, erosive forces ever carving out new meanders in the soft sediment.

Many of the shapes of the river valley are forged in times beyond even the span of the ancient oaks, when moving ice carved valleys from underlying rock and melt water scoured new shapes whilst also laying down a bed of softer geology upon it. Beneath the softer cover of familiar landforms lie the scars and moulding hand of deep geological time.

These timescales, from millennia to centuries, decades to years, months, days and even minutes, are nested within and co-dependent upon each other.

Geological land-forming processes provide habitat for centuries-old oaks, whose buds burst, leaves spread and then fall, and acorns disperse with the ebb and flow of the seasons. Migrant birds arrive from their travels for shelter within the embrace of the oak's robust branches, and to find necessary havens in which to feast, nest and depart. The same seemingly ageless boughs provide night-time refuge for flocks of fieldfares during their cyclic winter sojourn within our shores, and emergent leaves in the months of late spring and summer feed the larvae of the green hairstreak butterfly and other insects as well as providing daytime foraging for nuthatch and blue tit.

The synchrony of nature is intricate; way more complex and time-hewn than the orchestrated ticks of second, minute and hour hands and moon phases in the most sophisticated of human-made clocks. This marvellously evolved, life-supporting 'machine' of intimately interconnected and interdependent

timespans maintaining the functioning of the natural world is there for all to
see if we just pause to gaze and reflect upon it.

   In a human-made world of uncertainty and over-simplification, with
all its pressing stresses and exigencies, there before our eyes written in the
warp and weft of the floodplains and wider landscapes that give us home are
enduring certainties and complexities to amaze, inspire and calm.

MARCH

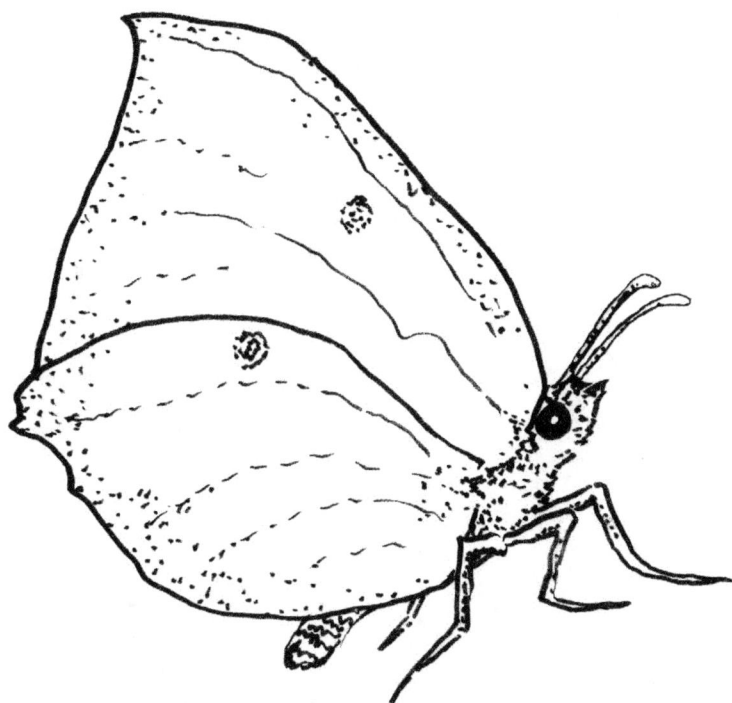

SPRINGTIME GOLD

WHILST NASCENT SPRING fights to prize the reluctant, icy grip of winter from earthen riverbanks, a splash of gold carrying the warm hues of full summer delights the eye.

Constellations of starry, sulphur-yellow celandine flowers may have been dotting the moist banks, some of them for weeks, and the soft yellow of early primroses may have begun to illuminate drier banks and hedgerows. But the rich gold splash of clustered florets of coltsfoot flowers, borne above the low sward by scaly and often purple-tinged, unbranched stems, has an opulent intensity that has the feeling of packaged warmth from summer yet to come.

Perhaps it is just me who feels this. After all, the coltsfoot was amongst the first wildflowers that I learned to name, along with bird's foot trefoil, daisy and dandelion, long ago on the Wealden clay of my early childhood.

But there is something almost magical about the explosion of vivid colour
of coltsfoot blooms bursting from muted earth, before even the leaves have
emerged. That, to me, marks out the coltsfoot as a true overture to the near
arrival of spring. The silver-white leaves, marked by angular teeth at their
margins, only appear after the flowers have set seed, and then lasting only a
short time before withering and dying in early summer. The florets themselves
generally occur in clusters as tight colonies of this perennial plant spread by
rhizomes, although the coltsfoot also reproduces by seeds.

The coltsfoot (*Tussilago farfara*), a member of the daisy family
Asteraceae, is not a scarce plant, favouring open and disturbed ground, most
commonly in moist and clay soils. The plant occurs widely across Europe and
north Africa as well as parts of western and central Asia as far as China and
the Russian Far East. It has also been introduced into the Americas, and it is
believed that this was at the hands of settlers due to its medicinal properties.
The plant spread there, and it is now common in both North and South
America.

The common name of the coltsfoot is attributed to the superficial
resemblance of the flower head to the foot of a colt. The plant enjoys a range
of alternative regional names that include ass's foot, bull's foot, foal's foot,
foalswort and horse foot. In Scotland, the name 'tushylucky' is still used.

Another regional name is coughwort. This name is reflected in the Latin
generic name *Tussilago*, derived from the two Latin words 'tussis' meaning
'cough' and 'ago' meaning 'to act on'. Coltsfoot extracts, as a tea, tincture or
syrup, have been widely used historically in herbal medicine to treat coughs,
colds and other respiratory disorders. Notable historic herbalists, including
Dioscorides and Pliny, recommended smoking coltsfoot to help the throat.
Although smoking is, in reality, unlikely to be of any great positive benefit
to respiratory health, coltsfoot is still thought in some places to be a useful
substitute for tobacco leading to another common name of the 'baccy plant'.
Other medicinal uses have included treatment of various conditions ranging
from skin and locomotor problems to viral infections, fever, rheumatism and
gout. More recently, some chemical constituents (particularly pyrrolozidine
alkaloids) of coltsfoot and related plants have led to concerns about these uses
and, in Germany, is the basis of a ban on the sale of coltsfoot.

The dry felt on the surface of coltsfoot leaves also smoulders well, so
coltsfoot has formerly been used as tinder. It is also reported that coltsfoot
was burned in certain magical rituals to create equilibrium, or else to call a

loved one back. Also, folklore from northern England that is now long-lost had it that coltsfoot leaves could be used to tell the future by using the shiny inner surface of the leaf, revealed when the thin outer layer of soft grey tissue was peeled off, as a window or mirror to reveal the future.

It is not just humans that appreciate the coltsfoot. The rhizomes of this plant bind and stabilise loose earthen soil, guarding against erosion. A range of insects, including both the gothic and the small angle shade moth, feed upon the leaves. Honeybees, bumblebees and other insects gather pollen and nectar from the flowers, important in early spring when other food sources are scarce and the emerging queen bees are most in need of food. As the seeds set with downy heads in April, they are favoured by goldfinches and some other birds for nest lining. Also, reportedly, Highlanders in years gone by used to gather these tufted coltsfoot seed heads as stuffing for bedding and mattresses.

The coltsfoot may be common on the earthen banks of our rivers, but they have meaning to wildlife and people alike, including as a symbol of new life emerging with the promise of growing day length and returning warmth.

WAGGING BY THE RIVER

T HE GREY WAGTAIL (*Motacilla cinerea*) is a slender, common bird found
year-round along our rivers. You may have seen this medium-sized bird
(up to nineteen centimetres, or about seven-and-a-half inches, in length) flitting
from floating rafts to low-hanging branches along stream edges, sometimes
singly but often in small groups. The bird has a high-pitched sharp call with a
song consisting of trills. It sings frequently.

Grey wagtails have a black head and a grey-white back with yellow
underneath, not to be confused with the wholly yellow body of the far scarcer
yellow wagtail (*Motacilla flava*). Breeding male grey wagtails have a black
throat edged by whitish moustachial stripes.

One of the more distinctive features of the grey wagtail is its long grey tail, which it has the habit of wagging up and down lending this genus of birds their common name. Indeed, the genus name *Motacilla* is a compound of the Latin *'motare'* ('to move about') and *'cilla'* ('tail').

Grey wagtails have a thin, dark bill, and a bright white eye-stripe. The thin bill is suited to the bird's habit of hunting the waterside for emerging flies and other small animal food items, potentially including tadpoles and snails. As such, it is a useful if simplistic indicator of river or stream health. These birds can also forage beside roads, particularly during the winter when they can also move to farms, gardens and towns. In fact, grey wagtails are considered partial migrants, freezing conditions driving them to seek warmer conditions further south potentially as far as North Africa.

Grey wagtails are naturally widely distributed across the Palearctic region – from western Europe including the British Isles, Scandinavia and the Mediterranean region, through eastern Europe and central Asia, along mountain ranges including the Urals and Himalayas, and extending eastwards to Korea and Japan – across which there are several reasonably distinct sub-species. Some occasionally turn up as vagrants in Alaska, and sometimes lower down in northern America.

The breeding season for grey wagtails is typically between April and July. Nests are built near fast-running streams or rivers, often between stones and roots or in manmade structures. Between three and six eggs are laid in a clutch. Multiple broods can be raised, as chicks typically fledge after about a fortnight following a two-week incubation period. Grey wagtails can live for up to eight years in the wild.

There are several theories as to why the three British species of wagtail (grey wagtail, yellow wagtail and the pied wagtail *Motacilla alba*) incessantly wag their tails. One theory is that it helps to flush out insects, though this is less likely as tail-wagging continues when the birds are resting or preening. Another theory is that it has a social function, including signalling to potential mates about overall condition, though this explanation may also not be valid as all ages and genders exhibit this behaviour. A further theory is that tail-wagging signals to potential predators that the bird is vigilant and unlikely to be caught, an explanation believed to be the case for some other animals. The truth may encompass combinations of any, all, or none of these theories!

Given this characteristic behaviour, it is not surprising that a mixed bag of myths has become associated with wagtails across Britain and Europe. In some cultures, they are seen as a sign of good luck, associated with the arrival of spring and a signal that the weather is getting warmer and the days are getting longer, and that they therefore bring good fortune to those who see them. In other localities in Britain, legend has it that wagtails are the souls of children who have died too young, returning to earth as wagtails to bring joy and happiness to others. In Ireland, a legend posits wagtails as the birds of the fairies, said to be able to see into the future and that they are used by the fairies to send messages to humans. In other parts of Europe, wagtails are regarded as a sign of bad news, associated with death and illness, and they are also said to be the birds of witches and fairies. In Sweden, there is a legend that wagtails are the birds of the sun, the only birds that can fly directly into the sun, and consequently seen as a symbol of hope and new beginnings.

Despite these mixed associations, wagtails are still popular birds in many parts of the world as they are generally regarded as graceful creatures with songs that are among the most beautiful.

INTERCONTINENTAL SOUP

A s temperatures and light levels rise in early spring, segueing into early summer, river gravels washed clean by winter spates often turn brown or green through the growth of algal films, filaments and other biological matter. As warm, dry conditions intensify as summer progresses, the water itself may take on a green or brownish hue as suspended algae proliferate in the barely stirred soup as river levels and currents decline further under high light intensities.

Whilst these seasonal trends are natural, the extremes we routinely now see in virtually all our lowland rivers are not. In part, this is caused by reduced dilution and less scouring by stronger flows as water is extracted for commercial and public supply at vast rates. Water is abstracted from surface flows but also from underground aquifers, robbing rivers of vital water even before it finds its way through to springs at the surface. But, in the main, the over-stimulation of algal growth is driven by enrichment of the water with nutrient chemicals, to the very substantial detriment of water purity and ecology.

What is a 'nutrient'? Many chemical elements are technically nutrients, used by and so stimulating biological activity. However, the term is more generally applied to what are technically known as 'micronutrient' substances – phosphorus and nitrogen amongst others – that are naturally scarce in soils and water, and so are limiting to the productivity of ecosystems.

As we know, we can add nutrients – be that in neat chemical form or as manure, compost or sewage residues – to a field or garden to stimulate the growth of crops, flowers or grass for grazing. However, the downside of this addition is that scarcer plants adapted to naturally lower-nutrient conditions tend to be out-competed by more vigorous 'weedy' species along with their associated complement of invertebrates and their predators. Conversion of naturally diverse, low-nutrient landscapes into intensively farmed fields enhances production of food and other biomass used by humans, but at the expense of wildlife richness. Also degraded are the many processes that natural ecosystems perform, including the storage and purification of water, the cycling of nutrients and carbon, hosting of pollinators and the predators of crop pests amongst other wildlife, and attractive landscapes.

The same principles apply to all ecosystems, and particularly so for rivers as the ultimate recipients of pressures across whole broad urban and rural landscapes.

So, where does all this enhanced input of nutrients come from?

In less intensely developed times with lower human population levels, we tended to live in a more circular manner. Food was grown locally to where it was consumed. Manure from animals, raised for traction, fur and hides, meat and dairy, was recirculated to cropland, pasture and meadow. Human wastes too, containing nutrients from locally produced crops and animals, also returned through productive reuse.

Wind forward to the modern era, and globalised trade amongst a human population now exceeding eight billion people changes that picture radically.

Basic nutrient chemicals are traded on an intercontinental basis, substantially for application in distant lands in purified forms as fertiliser. Morocco holds something like 70% of global phosphorus-rich rock reserves, with other significant exporting nations including Brazil, Canada, Finland, Russia, South Africa and Zimbabwe. Foodstuffs grown from these exported nutrients are also then traded globally, as are livestock feeds such as soybeans, often crossing not just nations but also continents. So, phosphorus mined in north Africa may fertilise soybeans in the Amazon basin that are then shipped as livestock feed to the UK or China where these nutrient chemicals are consumed and subsequently released, swamping natural re-assimilation processes.

We are inadvertently turning our wonderful rivers into an intercontinental soup of traded chemicals. Natural cycles are broken, the

resource of nutrient inputs resolving as pollutants that radically change
the utility and ecology of rivers. Excess nutrients also then accumulate
downstream in coastal seas, where excessive biological production and dying
organic matter decays to produce oxygen-depleted 'dead zones'. Whilst
some dead zones are natural, oceanographers noted increasing instances
and expanses of dead zones near inhabited coastlines since the 1970s, with
coastal regions such as the Baltic Sea, the northern Gulf of Mexico and the
Chesapeake Bay, as well as large enclosed water bodies such as Lake Erie
in north America, afflicted by depressed dissolved oxygen concentrations
due to excessive nutrient concentrations and consequently failing to support
aquatic life. An irony is that the world is running short of readily exploitable
phosphorus reserves but, at the same time, it has a growing legacy of aquatic
environments damaged by hyper-enrichment with excess nutrient chemicals.

You will, I am sure, have heard of policy language referring to a 'circular
economy'. Often, this is expressed as more recycling of end-of-life goods and
materials resulting in the generation of less waste, retaining more value in the
economy. But we need to look and act deeper – far deeper – to think about
how to restore our former, more sustainable circular habits with respect to our
interaction with food and other resources, and their implications for nutrient
chemicals, trade, and the vitality of soil and aquatic ecosystems essential to
sustain our needs into the future.

Clean and diverse rivers – with the intercontinental soups that ramify
our landscapes today relegated to a distant bad memory – would be a key
indicator of real progress towards this necessary goal.

RIVER ENGINEERING

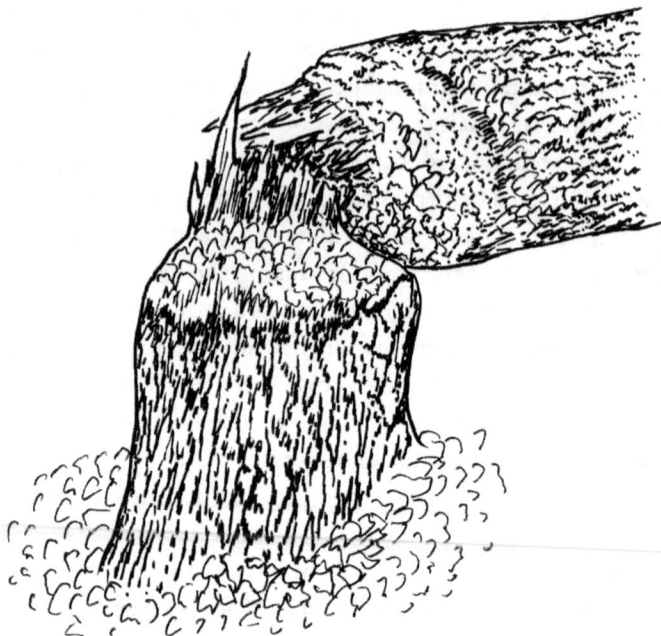

W E LIVE IN highly engineered landscapes, very remote from their
natural state.

Many classic romantic artworks portray bucolic British riverscapes. In
reality, most show river channels already separated from floodplains that
have been drained and denuded of the multiplicity of microhabitats – cut-off
channels, fens and wetland flushes, reedbeds, and so on – upon which many
species, particularly their early life stages, depend. Massive drainage and
conversion of flat valleys for agricultural, urban and industrial development,
starting from Roman times, gives us a distorted view of naturalness. Also,
by extension, we lack an objective frame of reference for what a healthy river
looks like.

Many of these artworks framing our subconscious vision also portray
rivers with additional heavy modification, including extensive impoundments
(locks, weirs and so on), bank modifications (such as wooden shuttering)
or significant livestock trampling. John Constable's famous painting 'The

Haywain' even has a horse-drawn truck trundling down the riverbed!

However, in a truly natural state, rivers were also heavily engineered. Some species are known as 'ecosystem engineers' as they are particularly influential in shaping the ecosystems of which they are part. A classic example is the action of beavers in modifying stream structure. Eurasian beavers (*Castor fiber*) were once widespread in Britain but were driven to extinction here in the 16th century. They have also suffered poorly over much of their former continental European range, mainly due to hunting for fur, meat and a glandular secretion known as 'castoreum' formerly used in perfumes, food and medicine.

The activities of beavers open areas of low tree cover in some places, creating biodiverse 'beaver meadows' (from where the name Beverley derives) promoting growth of fresh vegetation on which they feed. Felled wood is used to build dams impounding water, offering the beavers safety from predators, and fresh shoots are stored underwater to last these vegetarian animals throughout leaner winter months. Elsewhere in stream systems, outflows from dams tend to locally accelerate flows, flushing out sediment and opening up clean gravel spawning habitat for fish such as trout and salmon.

In recent years, beavers have been reintroduced locally in the UK, whether deliberately, accidentally or unauthorised, and have subsequently proliferated and spread. Re-established populations now are to be found in Scotland as well as in various locations across southern England. In England, the River Otter Beaver Trial is the only licenced population of free-living beavers, led by Devon Wildlife Trust working with Exeter University and subject to scientific studies since 2015. Other groups of beavers occur in scattered places across England, some resulting from escapes but many more apparently establishing after natural spread. After a decade of efforts to consent the release of beavers in Wales, the Welsh Government gave its backing in 2024 for the managed reintroduction of beavers to Welsh rivers.

Beaver reintroductions are not without public concern. Alarm is not infrequently expressed in local media about perceived problems associated with the reintroduction of beavers, with flooding often cited. Residents in Alyth, Perthshire (Scotland), expressed concern that upstream beaver dams might contribute to flooding of the town. However, scientific study comparing multiple beaver-modified and unmodified sites on headwater streams in eastern Scotland found that dam building by beavers held back water buffering stream flow and reducing flood risk downstream, whilst also restoring natural habitats and biodiversity and increasing other beneficial functions. This is corroborated by studies of the effects of beavers in large enclosures in southern England, which concluded that they significantly increased water storage and quality, naturally buffer flood risk, and yield multiple benefits for biodiversity. In fact, in southern England, many populations have remained largely undetected as they are shy animals, often burrowing in quiet places and not building the large dams that are associated with their larger American cousins.

In the west coast of America, restoration of populations of the far larger North American beaver (*Castor canadensis*) has had a positive influence on biodiversity through the creation and diversification of habitats, including creating ponds and wetlands, altering sediment transport processes and importing woody matter into aquatic environments. In particular, North American beaver introductions were found to enhance stream habitat beneficially for endangered Chinook and Steelhead salmon in the Upper Columbia River Basin in Eastern Washington, also providing nesting and foraging territory for passerine birds and improved habitat for bats.

In contemporary congested British landscapes, different places might be more or less appropriate for the spread or reintroduction of beavers. Their 'ecosystem engineering' activities can yield a multiplicity of linked benefits in many areas, particularly in upper catchments, as revealed by Scottish and English trials. Conversely, areas of commercial forestry, intensive farming, dense urban development encroaching on river edges, or where there are already bottlenecks in migratory fish passage may be less appropriate.

Whether we will or will not see a wider return of beavers to our local rivers is uncertain, though it is clear that they are spreading across Britain and in most cases without the dire consequences envisaged by popular media.

It is important to recognise that nature tends to engineer river ecosystems sympathetically with their natural processes, certainly more so than our efforts with diggers, concrete and steel!

THE TREES ARE SINGING

I S IT MUSIC, or is it noise? The sound of wind playing through trees is familiar to us all, and is particularly evident at night when the bustle of daytime activity is quieted. You can buy, or access online, recordings of the 'white noise' (it is actually 'pink noise') generated by the rush of wind through trees or generated by a waterfall. For many, this is a soothing, regenerating or soporific balm. These sounds even have their own name – 'psithurism' – and are certainly a respite from the harsher noises of busy society.

Is it music, noise or is it even language? An attuned ear can discern many distinctive messages embedded in this aerodynamic soundscape. The quivering rustle of aspen leaves, for example, can be recognised from far away, along with visual clues by day in the way that aspen leaves tremble with the passage of air. Both senses give the species its Latin name *Populus tremula*, literally 'fluttering or quavering poplar'. Other species too reveal their identities and condition through subtle acoustic signatures.

Forests speak to us in different tones depending on leaf type and season. The softer whisper of wind through the lush summertime foliage of deciduous trees morphs progressively through to a drier crackle as the leaves dry and wither into the autumn. Evergreen needles of finer profile by contrast 'shush' as they rub together more uniformly throughout the seasons. Friction against otherwise silent flows of air can be converted to whistles or howls through barren winter branches and twigs, or a coarser clatter as winds strengthen.

Other of the sounds of trees in the wind speak more of their distress. As the breeze strengthens, branches and twigs may creak as they rub. With growing energy, more violent movements may result in bark parting from underlying timber in places where it has formed to cover old wounds inflicted by trauma or the activities of animals of various types. The tree may recover as high winds abate, though lasting damage can also potentially occur.

Other acoustic phenomena that may be witnessed on cold nights following warm days under high-pressure meteorological conditions in winter are loud cracks. These are emitted as the chilling bark contracts and grates over inner timber that still carries warmth stored from the preceding day.

Trees, like all living things, respond to their environment, becoming stronger if exposed routinely to forceful winds. And, as we are all aware, persistent strong prevailing winds, such as those that occur commonly near the coast, sculpt them permanently.

But we live today in a changing climate. Perhaps all of us will have noted, and possibly remarked upon, how more frequently and violently storms now confront us. Where damaging forces beyond the normal range of extremes occur, boughs may be lost or split, or trees may be entirely toppled. In urban environments, this can cause severe damage to buildings and other infrastructure and assets though, in wilder settings, it may create space for natural regeneration and successional processes.

So, enjoy the diverse songs of the trees. Listen, and let them work their magic upon you, and maybe try to decipher the messages they convey. Though ostensibly largely inert, trees are very much living and actively interacting elements of our rich natural heritage with a unique language of their own.